THE ILLUSTRATED HISTORY OF
WORLD WAR TWO

AN AUTHORITATIVE AND DETAILED ACCOUNT OF THE MILITARY AND POLITICAL
EVENTS OF THE SECOND WORLD WAR, WITH OVER 350 PHOTOGRAPHS AND MAPS

INCLUDES SPECIAL FEATURES ON ALL OF THE MAJOR BATTLES AND CAMPAIGNS ON
LAND AND AT SEA, DETAILING MILITARY STRATEGIES, SUCCESSES AND FAILURES

DONALD SOMMERVILLE

southwater

This edition is published by Southwater,
an imprint of Anness Publishing Ltd,
Blaby Road, Wigston, Leicestershire LE18 4SE;
info@anness.com

www.southwaterbooks.com;
www.annesspublishing.com

Anness Publishing has a new picture agency outlet for images
for publishing, promotions or advertising. Please visit our
website www.practicalpictures.com for more information.

Publisher: Joanna Lorenz
Editorial Director: Helen Sudell
Editor: Elizabeth Young
Production Controller: Bessie Bai

Produced for Anness Publishing Ltd by Toucan Books

Toucan Books:
Managing Director: Ellen Dupont
Editor: Donald Sommerville
Project Manager: Hannah Bowen
Designer: Elizabeth Healey
Picture Researcher: Debra Weatherley
Cartographer: Julian Baker
Proofreader: Theresa Bebbington
Indexer: Michael Dent

ETHICAL TRADING POLICY
Because of our ongoing ecological investment programme,
you, as our customer, can have the pleasure and reassurance
of knowing that a tree is being cultivated on your behalf to
naturally replace the materials used to make the book you are
holding. For further information about this scheme, go to
www.annesspublishing.com/trees

Previously published as part of a larger volume, *The Complete
Illustrated History of World War II*

PUBLISHER'S NOTE
Although the advice and information in this book are
believed to be accurate and true at the time of going to press,
neither the authors nor the publisher can accept any legal
responsibility or liability for any errors or omissions that may
have been made.

Front cover clockwise from left: German troops parade in
Warsaw as part of a victory parade; Sir Winston Churchill
making the famed 'V' for 'Victory' sign. He is shown in the
uniform of the Royal Auxiliary Airforce. Ca. 1940-1945; bomb
damage in London; Hitler surveys campaign maps of the
Eastern Front with General Von Brauchitsch; US troops wade
ashore onto Utah beach, 6th June, 1944. Back cover,
clockwise from left: German troops in urban area; Admiral
Nimitz, V. Admiral Spruance with Major General Smith
USMC; Atom bomb cloud; German, Russian and US troops
meet on the Elbe River, 1945; British Home Guard, B
Company, 13th Battalion, Garrison, 1941; Johnny Johnson,
RAF fighter ace picturd in France 1944. Johnson was the top
scoring Western allied pilot against the Luftwaffe; A london
double decker bus which has been blow into a crater in
Balham London during the Blitz, October 1940; German
Infantryman, pictured during 1940-41. Front cover flap: 1944
D-Day – American troops in a landing craft huddle behind
the protective front. Back cover flap and page 3: British
Home Guard, B Company, 13th Battalion, Garrison, 1941.
Page 1: B-17 Flying Fortresses of the 'Mighty' Eighth Air
Force in flight over Eastern England 1944-45. Page 2: US 1st
Div. Troops disembarked from an LCVP landing craft wading
toward Omaha Beach on D-Day, June 6, 1944. Page 159: Sir
Winston Churchill making the famed 'V' for 'Victory' sign.

Contents

Timeline

World War II was truly a global conflict, with inter-related campaigns being fought simultaneously on land and in the air across vast areas of Europe, Asia and Africa and in every ocean.

1931–38

INTERNATIONAL EVENTS
Japan begins occupation of Manchuria (Sept 1931); Hitler becomes German Chancellor (Jan 1933); Italy invades Abyssinia (Oct 1935); Germany occupies Rhineland (Mar 1936); Italy annexes Abyssinia (May 1936); Japan invades China (July 1937); "Rape of Nanking" (Dec 1937); Germany annexes Austria (Mar 1938); Germany begins occupation of Czechoslovakia (Oct 1938)

1939

INTERNATIONAL EVENTS
Britain and France ally with Poland (Mar); Nazi–Soviet Pact agreed (23 Aug); Britain, France, Australia, India and New Zealand declare war on Germany (3 Sept); South Africa declares war on Germany (6 Sept); Canada declares war on Germany (10 Sept); US "Cash and Carry" law starts (Nov)
POLISH CAMPAIGN Germany invades Poland (1 Sept); USSR invades Poland (17 Sept); Warsaw captured (27 Sept); last Polish troops surrender (3 Oct)
RUSSO-FINNISH WAR USSR invades Finland (30 Nov)

1940

INTERNATIONAL EVENTS Italy declares war on France and UK (10 June); Baltic States seized by USSR (July); Italy, Germany and Japan agree Tripartite Pact (Sept); UK–USA "destroyers for bases" deal (Sept)
RUSSO-FINNISH WAR Ends with partial Soviet victory (12 Mar)
NORWAY AND DENMARK Germany invades (9 Apr); Allied resistance ends (9 June)
WESTERN FRONT Germany invades France and Low Countries (10 May); Dunkirk evacuation (26 May–4 June); French surrender (22 June)
BRITAIN Winston Churchill becomes Prime Minister (10 May); Battle of Britain (Aug–Sept); Blitz against British cities (Sept–May 1941)
UNITED STATES Conscription introduced (Sept); President Roosevelt re-elected (Nov)
BALKANS Italy invades Greece from Albania (Oct)
NORTH AFRICA Italy invades Egypt (Sept); British counter-attack begins (9 Dec)

1941

INTERNATIONAL EVENTS
Lend-Lease Act becomes law in USA (Mar); Japanese–Soviet neutrality agreement (Apr); Romania and Italy declare war on USSR (22 June); Japan's assets in USA frozen (July); USA and UK agree Atlantic Charter (12 Aug); UK declares war on Finland, Hungary and Romania; UK, USA and many other nations declare war on Japan (8 Dec); Germany and Italy declare war on USA (11 Dec)
BALKANS Germans conquer Yugoslavia (6–17 Apr); Germans conquer mainland Greece (6–30 Apr); Germans invade Crete (20 May–1 June)
NORTH AFRICA German troops arrive (Feb); British Crusader offensive begins (18 Nov)
EASTERN FRONT Germany invades USSR (22 June); Smolensk pocket eliminated (5 Aug); Kiev encirclement complete (19 Sept); German attack on Moscow starts (2 Oct); Moscow counter-offensive begins (5 Dec); Hitler takes over as Commander-in-Chief of German Army (19 Dec)
PACIFIC WAR Japan attacks Pearl Harbor (7 Dec); Japan attacks Malaya and Philippines (8 Dec)

1942

INTERNATIONAL EVENTS
United Nations Declaration issued by Allies (1 Jan)

HOLOCAUST Nazi Wannsee Conference plans "Final Solution" (20 Jan)
PACIFIC WAR Japanese capture Manila (2 Jan); Japanese capture Singapore (15 Feb); US troops surrender in Philippines (8 Apr); Battle of Coral Sea (7–9 May); Battle of Midway (4–6 June); US landings on Guadalcanal (7 Aug)
EASTERN FRONT Battle of Kharkov (15–27 May); Battle of Stalingrad begins (mid-Sept); Soviet counter-offensive near Stalingrad (19 Nov)
NORTH AFRICA Rommel attacks Gazala Line (26 May); Battle of El Alamein (23 Oct–4 Nov); Operation Torch begins (8 Nov)

1943

INTERNATIONAL EVENTS
Casablanca Conference, Allies announce unconditional surrender policy (14–24 Jan); Italy surrenders to Allies (8 Sept); Italy declares war on Germany (13 Oct); UK, USSR and USA meet in Teheran Conference (Nov–Dec)
PACIFIC WAR Allied landings on New Georgia (20 June); US landings in Gilbert Islands (20 Nov)
EASTERN FRONT German surrender at Stalingrad (2 Feb); Battle of Kursk begins (5 July); Kiev falls to Soviets (6 Nov)

NORTH AFRICA Battle of Kasserine (14–24 Feb); Axis surrender in Tunisia (13 May)
ITALY Invasion of Sicily (10 July); capture of Sicily complete (17 Aug); Salerno landings (9 Sept)

1944

INTERNATIONAL EVENTS
Romania agrees armistice with Allies, declares war on Germany (23 & 25 Aug); Bulgaria surrenders (8 Sept); Finland agrees armistice (10 Sept)
EASTERN FRONT End of siege of Leningrad (27 Jan); Soviets capture Minsk (3 July); Warsaw Rising (1 Aug–2 Oct); Partisans liberate Belgrade (20 Oct)
MEDITERRANEAN Allied landings at Anzio (22 Jan); Rome liberated (4 June); British liberate Athens (14 Oct)
WESTERN FRONT D-Day (6 June); Normandy breakout (1 Aug); landings in southern France (15 Aug); Allies capture Antwerp (4 Sept); Operation Market-Garden (17–26 Sept); Battle of Bulge begins (16 Dec)
PACIFIC Battle of Philippine Sea (19–20 June); landings on Leyte (20 Oct); Battle of Leyte Gulf (24–6 Oct)
BURMA Battles of Imphal and Kohima (Mar–July)

1945

INTERNATIONAL EVENTS
Roosevelt dies, Truman becomes President of USA (12 Apr); Hitler commits suicide (30 Apr); Germans surrender in: Italy (2 May), north Germany (4 May), sign overall surrender (7 May); VE-Day (8 May); Potsdam Conference (17 July–2 Aug); Attlee becomes UK Prime Minister (26 July); USSR declares war on Japan (8 Aug); Japan agrees surrender (14 Aug); VJ-Day (15 Aug); Japan signs surrender (2 Sept)
WESTERN FRONT Allies cross Rhine at Remagen (7 Mar); US and Soviet troops meet on Elbe (25 Apr)
EASTERN FRONT Soviets take Warsaw (17 Jan); Vienna falls to Soviets (13 Apr); fighting ends in Berlin (2 May); last German troops surrender in Czechoslovakia (13 May)
BURMA British capture Mandalay (20 Mar); British capture Rangoon (3 May)
PACIFIC Landings on Luzon (9 Jan); landings on Iwo Jima (19 Feb); landings on Okinawa (1 Apr); A-bomb attack on Hiroshima (6 Aug); Soviet attack in Manchuria and A-bomb attack on Nagasaki (9 Aug)

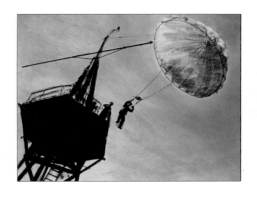

Troubled Times: USA and USSR Soviet paratroop training during the 1930s.

Failing Economies A disabled war veteran begging in the streets of Berlin in the 1920s.

Fascism and Nazism Horst Wessel, later lauded as a martyr in the Nazi cause, on parade in 1929.

APPROACH TO WAR

World War I – the "war to end all wars" – had been centred in Europe but in fact it solved few of Europe's problems. Indeed, it established other problems that the dictators and militarists of the 1930s would exploit to achieve their ends, or so they hoped – but instead this went on to create a new and more terrible conflict.

WWI had been the most costly conflict in human history, both in terms of loss of life and in physical destruction. Not only the killing but the whole process of war production had been thoroughly mechanized and industrialized. Previous standards of humane conduct in types of weapons used and the involvement of civilians were also quickly disregarded. World War II would take all these trends to new extremes.

Germany's ability to dominate Europe had not been removed by WWI. The public will for this to happen remained a force in German life, not just for Hitler and his fellow fascists. Similarly, Japan's leaders, victorious Allies in WWI, came to feel that they had been denied their just rewards and that their national destiny was being circumscribed by racist Europeans and Americans. In these tough economic times, other nations failed to respond well to such issues. Some chose isolationism, others negotiation – and its feeble cousin appeasement – backed by a half-hearted rearmament. When faced with enemies who were happy to start wars whenever it suited them, these strategies were inadequate.

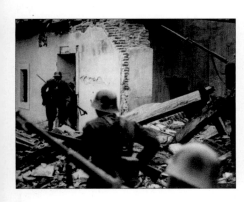

Troubled Times: Western Europe Nationalist troops in Madrid during the Spanish Civil War.

Fascism and Nazism Mussolini (wearing red sash) seized power in Italy in 1922.

Troubled Times: USA and USSR Josef Stalin's purges gravely weakened the USSR in the 1930s.

The Legacy of World War I

The peace settlement that ended the Great War stored up many problems for the future. The former Anglo-French Commander-in-Chief, Marshal Ferdinand Foch, made the best assessment: "This is not a treaty. It is an armistice for twenty years."

The victorious Allies came to Paris for the negotiation of the treaties to end World War I determined to prevent a repetition of the conflict. However, the steps they took to achieve this proved to be ill-judged. Separate treaties were agreed with each of the former Central Powers (usually referred to as the Treaty of Versailles, however, in fact this was the one concluded with only Germany). The three most powerful victors (the USA, Britain and France) dominated the negotiations, though representatives from many other Allied countries were also present.

However, the leaders of the new USSR and the old Russia were still fighting a destructive and divisive civil war and were not included in talks. Also absent were representatives of

Below: Anti-communist White Russian cavalry in action during the Russian Civil War of 1919–21.

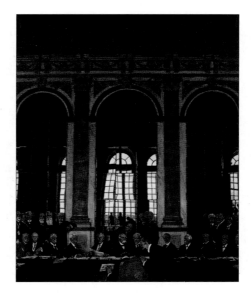

Above: The signing of the Treaty of Versailles in the Hall of Mirrors at the palace of Versailles.

the defeated Central Powers; they would be summoned to sign once the text of the treaties had been agreed but had no say in negotiations. These absences were the source of the first great weakness of the Versailles settlement: in Germany, in particular, it would be characterized in

years to come as the "Dictate of Versailles" and therefore by definition was rejected as unjust.

A NEW EUROPE

The treaties redrew the map of Europe, which again stored up trouble for the future. The Austro-Hungarian Empire was cut apart: Austria and Hungary became separate nations and two new nations, Czechoslovakia and Yugoslavia, were founded. Romania took territory from Hungary and Bulgaria, while the Baltic States became independent, largely being created from the Russian Empire. So, too, was Poland, which also included a former German province and, more controversially, gained access to the sea via the "Polish Corridor" at Danzig. This split the main part of Germany from the province of East Prussia. France regained Alsace and Lorraine, taken by Germany after the Franco-Prussian War of 1870–1. Belgium and even Denmark also gained former German territory. In all Germany lost 13 per cent of its pre-war area, while its colonies became possessions of one or other of the Allies.

Germany's armed forces were to be reduced to a fraction of their previous size. To add yet more resentment, Germany had to accept a clause stating that the war had been entirely its fault (which was far from true) and that Germany must therefore pay substantial financial reparations for the damage and destruction caused. The size of the bill was to be fixed later.

GROWING RESENTMENT

There were many problems with all this, not just in the anger stored up in Germany at what were in many ways real injustices. Almost none of the new nations had an ethnically homogeneous population and most were unhappy with where their borders had been set. Although Britain and France were obviously the most powerful European nations, having

Above: The German battle-cruiser *Hindenburg* scuttled by its crew in protest over the peace negotiations.

suffered so much in the war and with problems of their own they were unwilling to take the lead in making the settlement work.

To perform such a role a new international body, the League of Nations, was set up, largely at the urging of the USA's President Woodrow Wilson. However, it remained to be

seen how well it would function and, sadly, from the beginning it was limited by the refusal of the US Congress to allow the USA to join.

None of this made World War II inevitable, or anything like it, but anger at the way Germany had been treated did inspire an ex-corporal called Adolf Hitler to join a tiny radical political group named the German Workers' Party in Munich in September 1919.

Below: French troops occupying Essen in the Rhineland in 1919.

THE WASHINGTON NAVAL TREATY

Japan, one of the Allied powers in WWI, felt that it had not been adequately rewarded for its efforts because the Versailles Treaty granted it little more than a handful of former German islands in the Pacific. By the early 1920s a naval arms race had developed, with Japan, the USA and Britain all making plans for fleets of new and huge battleships, which in truth no one really wanted or could afford. In February 1922 these three, along with France and Italy, agreed the Washington Treaty to limit their future naval forces. The Japanese, in particular, were reluctant signatories and would come to believe that, yet again, they had been swindled of their just status by a racist conspiracy of Anglo-Saxons. Although the Treaty and later successors would remain in force until the late 1930s, this became another source of trouble for the future.

Failing Economies

The world economy had been left unbalanced by the debts owed both by the victors and the losers after WWI, and national leaders, with little idea how to manage their domestic economies, were unable to respond effectively to the problems this caused.

The years immediately after WWI saw many hardships and political problems for people all around the world, not just in defeated Germany. Both the Nazi Party and Italian Fascism had their origins in this period. Then, after a period of growing prosperity and seeming progress toward international amity, the collapse of American share prices in 1929 ushered in the Great Depression and an era of political turmoil.

In all the former warring countries, ex-soldiers had to find their way back into civil society but did not always find jobs easy to come by; the many disabled veterans found life particularly difficult.

Poverty was an everyday reality for millions of war widows and orphans. Those higher up the social scale worried that the

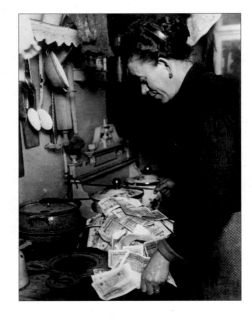

Above: A German housewife uses worthless paper money to light her stove during the 1923 crisis.

Below: Having left Germany when the Versailles Treaty was signed, French troops returned in 1923 when reparations payments were delayed.

turmoil of Russia's communist revolution might spread. In Germany right-wingers formed militias to fight socialists and revolutionaries, and in Britain and other countries troops clashed in the streets with strikers and other protesters.

With its economic struggles, Germany fell behind in its reparations payments. In retaliation French and Belgian troops occupied the Ruhr in January 1923, an action that triggered a financial crisis and massive inflation in Germany. By late 1923 the mark's foreign exchange value was 130 billion to the dollar. In Germany money was virtually worthless paper and many in the middle classes saw their savings wiped out.

AMERICAN LOANS

In 1924 an Allied committee, which was led by American banker Charles Dawes (shortly to become US Vice-President), set up a new plan for Germany's reparations payments, which brought stability and growth to the German economy (but only on the back of US loans). Other countries were also heavily indebted to the USA for loans raised during WWI; they, too, struggled to repay these because of a decline in international trade, partly caused by the USA's protectionist measures.

For the moment, however, the American economy and stock market were booming, while in international affairs

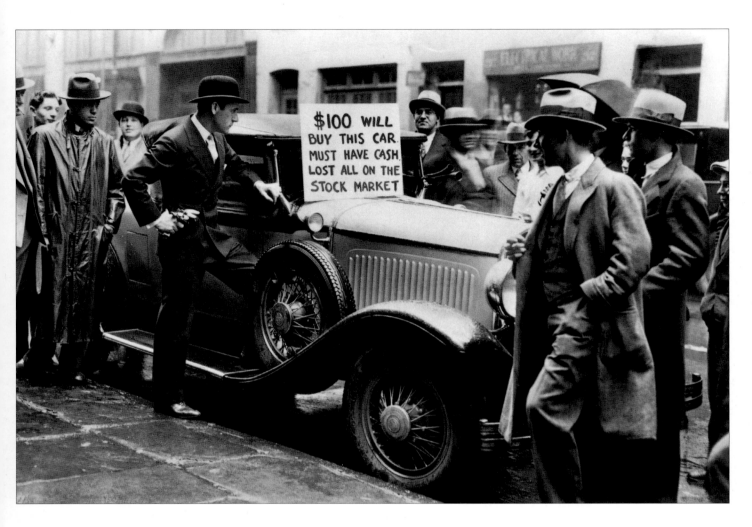

Above: Fooled by steadily rising returns through the 1920s, many Americans speculated on the stock market and had to pay the price.

there seemed to be other promising signs. In 1926 Germany joined the League of Nations and seemed to be reasonably stable in its domestic politics, even though radical parties of both left and right had significant followings.

In 1928 a range of leading nations even signed a treaty – called the Kellogg–Briand Pact (after the US secretary of state and the French foreign minister who led the negotiations) – by which they agreed to renounce the use of aggressive war as an instrument of national policy. Obviously, this agreement did not fulfil its aims, but

it has remained important in international law. It would be used after WWII to support a number of the charges made against the leaders of Germany and Japan by the International War Crimes Tribunals.

Below: A street scene in the early 1920s, in fact in Berlin but with equivalents in many places.

In 1929 a plan proposed by Owen Young, another American banker, finally fixed the amount of war reparations Germany still had to pay. Though the terms were milder than those previously in force, many Germans still believed they were overly harsh, even if they allowed this issue finally to be closed.

ECONOMIC COLLAPSE

Then, in October 1929, prices collapsed on New York's Stock Exchange and the credit that had financed the USA's own economic growth and kept many foreign economies healthy dried up. Soon there would be millions of unemployed in all industrialized nations and great opportunities for politicians offering radical solutions to these problems.

Fascism and Nazism

In Italy, and then in Germany, radical political movements with dominating leaders took control of the governments and then the whole of national life, remaking these countries in a new, violent, intolerant and ultra-nationalist form.

Both Italy and Germany saw much use of violence to suppress strikes and socialist activities immediately after WWI. In Italy the National Fascist Party, which was led by journalist and war veteran Benito Mussolini, was prominent in these activities. Backed by numerous party thugs (*squadristi*, or Blackshirts), Mussolini took advantage of continuing political instability to have himself appointed Prime Minister in 1922. Then, in 1924–5, a further crisis (caused by the Blackshirt murder of a leading socialist) saw Mussolini discard the pretence of constitutional rule and begin the process of making Italy a fascist state.

Below: A Nazi parade in 1929, led by Horst Wessel, later celebrated as a martyr in the Nazi cause.

Above: Mussolini (wearing sash), during the 1922 "March on Rome" when he seized power in Italy.

FASCIST RULE

Mussolini's message was ultra-nationalist and stated that the good of the nation came before any individual rights or liberties. Elections were first rigged and then abolished, as were political parties and freedom of speech; fascist organizations were set up in every walk of life, starting with one for boys of six and upward. Mussolini himself became *Il Duce* ("the leader") and took unchallenged control of the government, supported by propaganda that claimed, among other things: "Mussolini is always right."

Hitler's rise to power in Germany followed a similar though rather longer route. After building his tiny political party, renamed the National Socialist German Workers' Party, into a significant local force, Hitler mounted an attempted coup in Munich in 1923. This "Beer Hall Putsch" failed and Hitler was jailed for a time. However, he did gain a national reputation from this event – one of his co-conspirators was General Erich Ludendorff, one of Germany's most famous soldiers in WWI.

In jail Hitler wrote his political manifesto *Mein Kampf* (usually translated as "My Struggle"), which set out very clearly the core of his beliefs: a hatred of Jews and communists and an intention to gain new territory for the German race in eastern Europe (*Lebensraum*, or "living space").

NAZIS IN POWER

Hitler and his party remained fairly minor players until the world economic crash began in 1929. Now allied with big business interests and preaching that Germany's ills were caused

ADOLF HITLER

Hitler (1889–1945) alone did not cause WWII, but he did more than anyone else to bring it about. His ideas and plans shaped the war's character, helping make it the most brutal conflict in human history. Hitler, an Austrian by birth, fought as a German soldier in WWI and went into politics shortly after, disgusted by the outcome of the war. His political views were based on anti-communism and anti-semitism, and a sense of his own and Germany's destiny to rule. His regime was chaotic and, as time went by, his orders were increasingly irrational. He was as responsible for Germany's ruinous defeat in 1945, as he had been for the astonishing successes of the early war years.

Right: Hitler and members of his cabinet following his appointment as chancellor in January 1933.

from abroad and by the detested Treaty of Versailles, Hitler found substantial new support.

In 1932 the Nazis became the largest party in the Reichstag (Germany's parliament). After further elections and some complicated political manoeuvring, Hitler was then appointed as chancellor at the head of a multi-party government by President Hindenburg in January 1933.

By late 1934, after Hindenburg's death, Hitler had taken complete control and ruled with legally acquired emergency powers. He became the *Führer* ("leader"), combining the offices of president and chancellor; all opposition political parties were banned; concentration camps, the Gestapo secret police and the rest of the apparatus of a police state were established; and the members of Germany's armed forces all swore a loyalty oath to Hitler personally.

In 1934 Hitler also confirmed his own supremacy within the Nazi movement in the "Night of the Long Knives". The party's left-wingers and the leader of the party militia (the SA or Brownshirts) were among those killed. The SS, led by Heinrich Himmler, became more important. Legal persecu-tion of Germany's Jews began in earnest with the Nuremberg Laws of 1935, which withdrew many civil rights. At the same time Jews suffered increasingly from thuggery and intimidation.

Below: Nazi thugs making an example of "criminals" – a Jew and his Christian girlfriend.

Aggression: Europe and Asia

Throughout the 1930s first Japan, then Italy and finally Germany sought territorial gains by violent means. They backed their aggression with a ruthlessness seldom seen in international affairs and with new and powerful armaments.

World War II began, some would say, in September 1931, when Japan attacked and in effect annexed the Chinese province of Manchuria. The attack was inspired by a conspiracy of middle-ranking Japanese Army officers who faked a sabotage incident on the South Manchurian Railway, owned by the Japanese. The government in Tokyo knew nothing of this but went along with events when a full-scale advance was immediately started. Throughout the approach to war both the Japanese Army and Navy (and factions within them) would in effect be laws unto themselves.

In February 1932 Manchuria was declared independent by the Japanese as Manchukuo, but in reality it was a puppet state economically exploited

Below: German troops crossing the Rhine bridge into Cologne in March 1936, Hitler's first advance.

Above: Japanese troops march into Nanking in December 1937.

under Japanese control. In 1933 when a League of Nations investigation finally stated what was obvious (that Japan was the aggressor), Japan simply left the League and increased its military budget.

THE NAZI THREAT

Hitler also left the League in 1933 – ostensibly because other countries had refused to disarm

to Germany's level, but the reality was different. In 1935 he reintroduced compulsory military service and announced the existence of a German air force, both outright violations of the Treaty of Versailles. Britain, France and, at this stage, Italy condemned these moves but this was a sham. Later the same summer, without prior consultation with France, Britain concluded the Anglo-German Naval Agreement, specifically allowing expansion of the German Navy and the creation of a U-boat force.

Italy was the next to make a move. Aware of the country's modest resources, Mussolini's government had not sought gains abroad in the first decade of fascist rule, though it had brutally consolidated control

Below: Puyi, Chinese puppet ruler of Manchukuo, attends a ceremony with his Japanese backers.

over Italy's existing colonies in Africa. However, in October 1935, Italy attacked Abyssinia. By May 1936 it had completed the annexation, despite half-hearted sanctions introduced by the League of Nations.

Encouraged by this, in March 1936 Hitler sent troops into the Rhineland area, demilitarized by the Versailles terms. Again, all Britain and France could muster were brief protests. Hitler made his move despite opposition from his generals. By being proved right, his control over them was made more secure and his belief in his own military judgement confirmed.

In February 1938 he completed his hold over his armed forces by dismissing the two top generals, the war minister and the commander-in-chief, taking over the supreme command himself. In March 1938 the next step was to merge Austria into Germany, sending troops across the border after Austrian Nazis had destabilized the government. Clearly, this was not going to be his last target.

WAR IN CHINA

With the establishment of Manchukuo, there had been various clashes between the Japanese Kwantung Army there and the Chinese across the border in northern China. In July 1937 the Kwantung Army (not under control from Tokyo), used an exchange of shots near the Marco Polo Bridge on the outskirts of Beijing as an excuse for escalation. There was heavy fighting around Shanghai for several months from August, before the Japanese made their move inland to Nanjing (then usually known as Nanking) in

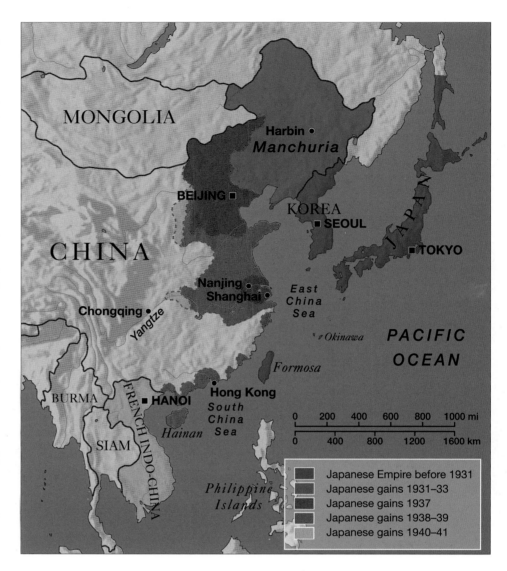

CHINA AND MANCHURIA
Japan's annexation of Manchuria and advance into China up to December 1941.

December. When they captured the city the Japanese forces went on a rampage of murder, looting and rape for several days. This "rape of Nanking" was reported around the world and widely condemned.

Although stronger than it had previously been, Jiang Jieshi's (Chiang Kai-shek's) Nationalist Chinese government could not prevent the Japanese, with more than a million men deployed, taking control of much of northern and eastern China over the next two years.

Above: German tanks parade through Vienna in 1938, after Austria's *Anschluss* with Germany.

Troubled Times: USA and USSR

The 1930s were times of social, political and economic upheaval in the USA and USSR. In their very different ways both countries failed to develop effective responses to the new challenges from Germany and Japan.

In the 1930s the USA and the USSR were not the super-powers they became after WWII. As well as being pre-occupied with economic difficulties, and political controversy over how to respond, the American people were unsure what their country's role in the world ought to be: should they participate fully or were they better off if they stood apart?

For its part the USSR was rent through the decade by a range of self-inflicted wounds as the economy was completely reworked and the rule of Josef Stalin and the Communist Party became yet more brutal and unchallengeable.

THE UNITED STATES

President Franklin Roosevelt was inaugurated in March 1933 with a quarter of the US work-force unemployed and the gross national product half that of the late 1920s. His New Deal poli-cies encompassed a range of measures: of public works, wel-fare and poor relief, reform of the banking system and more. For Roosevelt and the American people the priority for the remainder of the decade would always be domestic concerns.

His achievements delighted some Americans while others despised him. Economists remained unsure how effective many of his policies were, but there was no doubt that he greatly enhanced the power and prestige of the presidency in ways that would become impor-tant in the following decade.

Most Americans agreed that their nation had blundered unwisely into war in 1917 and felt that their country should avoid future conflicts, especially in Europe. The USA had refused to join the League of Nations in 1919. In 1935, and again in 1937, Congress passed neutrality laws to try to ensure

Above: The Tennessee Valley Authority (TVA) was one of Roosevelt's New Deal initiatives.

that the USA was not again dragged into war. In any case the USA had comparatively little military muscle. The US Navy was indeed a world force, allowed by treaty to be equal in size with the British Royal Navy. However, only with re-armament measures at the end of the 1930s did it actually build up to its permitted level. In addition, the US Army was so small as to be internationally irrelevant. Nothing in all this was likely to deter aggression.

THE USSR

Throughout the 1930s the USSR was as inward-looking and in an even deeper state

Left: Strikers and police clash at a Michigan car plant in 1937, a common sight in 1930s' USA.

of turmoil than the USA. The government's policies of mass industrialization and the collectivization of peasant farms were pushed through. On one hand they created the industrial base that could withstand Hitler's attack in 1941, but on the other the cost was huge, with up to 15 million people dead from murder and famine in the rural areas.

All opposition, whether real or imagined, to the rule of the Communist Party was crushed in the so-called Great Terror, with millions of citizens being shipped off to the brutal labour camps of the Siberian GULag. During this terrifying process the state became governed not by the dictatorship of the proletariat, as provided for in Marxist-Leninist theory, but by the absolute rule of one man: Josef Stalin.

The USSR's huge military potential was clear. Soviet forces had pioneered experiments – in paratroop operations, for example – and later in the decade Marshal Mikhail Tukhachevsky was working to create new tank formations, similar to those that would soon be seen in Germany. In addition, the process of industrialization saw both the quantity and quality of military equipment greatly improve by the late 1930s.

Tukhachevsky, however, and most senior commanders as well as about half the junior officers were all executed during the Terror. Their replacements, Stalin's creatures, like all senior officials, were slow to repair the damage done. Consequently, the USSR was not at all well prepared for the coming war.

JOSEF STALIN

Stalin (1879–1953) was the dictator who ruled the USSR with an increasingly tight grip after the death of Lenin in 1924 and who would extend his control to cover all of eastern Europe by the end of the war. He tolerated no rivals or expressions of dissent. His paranoia was so extreme that millions of loyal Soviet citizens were murdered or sent to the GULag slave-labour camps. His cold and cynical calculations led him astray in 1941 when he refused to prepare properly for Hitler's attack, but otherwise his ruthless energy drove his country forward to victory and the establishment of a new European empire.

Below: Stalin, with Molotov (left), foreign minister throughout WWII, and Marshal Voroshilov, a poor general but a favoured crony of his leader.

Below: Three out of five Soviet marshals were executed in Stalin's Great Terror, including Mikhail Tukhachevsky (shown here).

Below: Soviet paratroop experiments. After the Terror generals reverted to traditional infantry-based tactics.

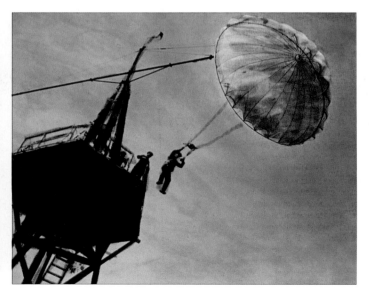

Troubled Times: Western Europe

Britain and France had played the main part in defeating German aggression in WWI, but their casualties and economic and social problems left them with diminished resources and little will to repeat the process.

In the inter-war years many British people saw WWI as an aberration. They thought that in foreign affairs Britain was an imperial and maritime power and should concentrate on those aspects. Sending a mass conscript army to fight and die in a continental war was not something Britain historically had been accustomed to do and should be reluctant to repeat, especially since it became increasingly clear that the Versailles Treaty had not come close to solving Europe's problems. British resources had been plundered to win WWI and in the economic crisis of the 1930s, British governments could see no way of standing up to Hitler

Below: The first meeting, in 1920, of the Council of the League of Nations, the body roughly equivalent to the later UN Security Council.

Left: Stanley Baldwin, three-times British Prime Minister in the 1920s and '30s, was slow to rearm in the face of Hitler's threats.

in Europe, if at the same time they had to protect the British Empire against Japan.

There was also a strong feeling in some quarters that the Versailles settlement had indeed been unjust. Some also felt that a Germany restored to a more realistic international status under Hitler's leadership

could at least be relied on to help keep the communist menace confined to the USSR.

Overall, Britain avoided co-operating closely with France until 1939. This had the dual effect of preventing another "continental commitment" and also preserving relations with the dominion nations of the Empire, which were reluctant to become involved in Europe's troubles once again. Britain's failure to work with France was shown in 1935, for example. In April that year Britain joined France and Italy in a conference at Stresa to condemn Germany's breaches of the Versailles Treaty – then two months later unilaterally and totally hypocritically negotiated the Anglo-German Naval Agreement, which specifically allowed Germany to make further breaches.

FRENCH RELUCTANCE

The human and physical cost of WWI for France had been vast. Even before the war France's population had been overtaken by that of Germany and the French economy was nowhere near as solid. Continued demographic and economic weakness in the inter-war years went hand in hand with political instability. Successive insecure governments formed and re-formed.

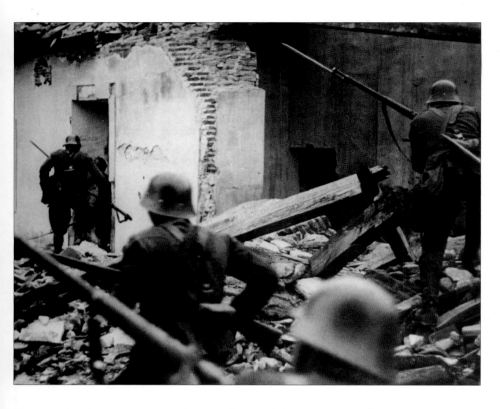

France had gone to war in 1914 with a wholeheartedly offensive outlook. However, by the 1930s, the situation had changed and any sort of military response in a crisis was out of the question – unless France could muster overwhelming and enthusiastic international support.

ABYSSINIA AND SPAIN

Italy's invasion of Abyssinia in 1935 gave the first clear demonstration of how enfeebled Britain and France had become. Already Japan had proved the weakness of the League of Nations by simply walking out and carrying on regardless when the annexation of Manchuria was condemned. British- and French-led League sanctions against Italy for attacking Abyssinia were hardly stringent – oil supplies were not stopped and Italian troopships were still allowed to use the Suez Canal. Sanctions were abandoned in less than a year after the Italians had overrun Abyssinia.

Italy and Germany had been brought closer by the opposition their various measures had met, ineffective though it had been. This process was confirmed, in part, by the next major development: the Spanish Civil War, which began in July 1936.

Both Germany and Italy sent significant help to Spain's right-wing Nationalist rebels. The Soviets sent less valuable help to Spain's Republicans, but France's leftist Popular Front government refused assistance. Britain condemned foreign interference in Spain's affairs but took virtually no action to back their words up.

The war was also important for the lessons major armies drew from it. France and the Soviets concluded that tanks were less effective in battle than some had thought; Germany saw things differently, in particular using Spain as the testing ground for new air-combat and ground-support techniques.

Below: Italian ships pass through the British-controlled Suez Canal, demonstrating the weakness of League of Nations sanctions in 1936.

THE MAGINOT LINE

Named after André Maginot, the French minister of war who started its construction in 1930, this was a deep and sophisticated system of fortification all along the Franco-German border. Built in line with the overall defensive nature of French strategy, work on it continued through the decade. Blockhouses, anti-tank defences, strong points, major forts and more were all built at a cost of several billion francs. However, the major weakness was that the defences, strong as they were, did not extend to cover the whole of France's northern border.

Europe on the Brink

Prime Minister Chamberlain proclaimed "peace for our time" when he returned from Munich, but the reality was that 1938 and 1939 saw Hitler's relentless expansionism drive Europe into a new and terrible war.

Czechoslovakia had been created by the Versailles Treaty. By 1938 about a third of its population were German speakers who lived principally in the border area known as the Sudetenland. For some time the Sudeten German Party, with Nazi support, had been agitating for union with Germany, and in September 1938 there was a new crisis, provoked by Hitler.

Although the Czechoslovak authorities soon had control of the situation, Britain's Prime Minister Neville Chamberlain decided there needed to be a permanent solution to the problem. It would probably have been wise if Britain and France had stood firm and risked war to help Czechoslovakia: the Czech

Below: Joachim von Ribbentrop, Hitler's foreign minister, signs the Nazi–Soviet Pact. Stalin and Molotov smile in the background.

Above: From left, Chamberlain, Daladier (French premier), Hitler and Mussolini at Munich in 1938.

military and its border defences were very strong and the German armed forces far less prepared for war than was later the case. Instead, although France was resigned to fighting, Chamberlain chose to negotiate.

MUNICH AGREEMENT

Chamberlain flew to Munich to meet Hitler, to negotiate a deal to force Czechoslovakia to cede to Germany areas where the majority of the people were ethnic Germans. Without British support, France had little option but to abandon the Czechs as well. In return Chamberlain had Hitler sign a vague friendship agreement and, on his return, announced that he had secured "peace for our time". He seems to have thought that, fundamentally, Hitler was a reasonable statesman who would keep his word – if that were the case, Czechoslovakia's problems were

a local issue not worth provoking another European war over – a war that Britain could not fight without jeopardizing its Empire in the Far East, which was increasingly under threat from the Japanese.

In early October 1938 Germany moved into the Sudetenland and the remainder of Czechoslovakia was split into three autonomous provinces. Then Poland, followed by Hungary, also grabbed disputed areas over the next weeks. In March 1939 Hitler moved in to complete the destruction of Czechoslovakia.

By that point Britain and France were ready to do a little more so they issued a guarantee of support to Poland, which was clearly Hitler's next target. The international status of the city of Danzig (Gdansk), and the Polish Corridor that divided East Prussia from the main part of Germany, had long been seen as an affront to German nationalism. Now Hitler vehemently demanded their return.

Right: Nazis on parade in Danzig (Gdansk) in 1939. Their banner proclaims "Danzig is a German town".

NAZI–SOVIET PACT

With Hitler now looking east, the USSR's position became more important. In the summer of 1939 Britain and France half-heartedly began talks in Moscow. However, these made little progress when it became clear that for Stalin any alliance was conditional on having the right to station troops in Poland.

Instead, in mid-August, the world was stunned when the communists and Nazis, formerly implacable enemies, became friends with the signing of the Soviet–German Non-Aggression Pact.

What the rest of the world did not know was that secret parts of this deal provided for Poland to be divided up between Russia and Germany

and that the Baltic States and Finland would also lose their independence to Russia.

Earlier that summer Britain and France had finally begun military co-operation planning, and Britain had introduced conscription in May. Even at this last moment Chamberlain was still looking for some compromise concession to Hitler that might avoid war.

When a formal Anglo-Polish alliance treaty was announced on 25 August, Hitler hesitated for a few days, postponing Germany's planned attack on Poland from 26 August to 1 September – but at dawn that morning the invasion began.

GERMAN EXPANSION, 1936–9
Poland and Hungary also joined in the partition of Czechoslovakia.

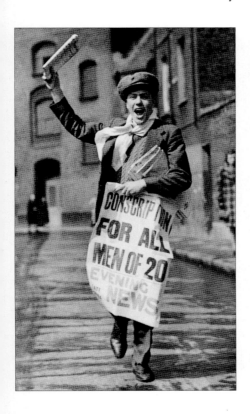

Above: The announcement of conscription in Britain in May 1939.

Tanks, 1939–42 An early model German Panzer 3 during a river-crossing operation.

Air Combat: Weapons, Tactics and Aces The ball turret of a B-17 Flying Fortress.

Anti-tank Guns, 1939–42 A Soviet 45mm M1937 anti-tank gun coming under artillery fire.

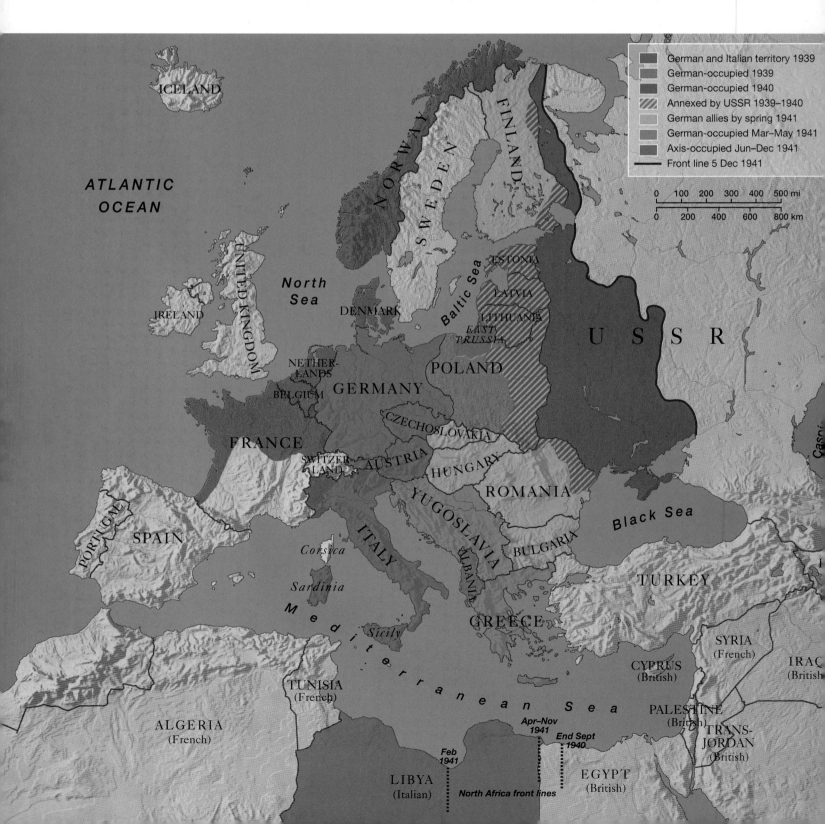

German and Italian territory 1939
German-occupied 1939
German-occupied 1940
Annexed by USSR 1939–1940
German allies by spring 1941
German-occupied Mar–May 1941
Axis-occupied Jun–Dec 1941
Front line 5 Dec 1941

0   100   200   300   400   500 mi
0   200   400   600   800 km

ICELAND

ATLANTIC OCEAN

NORWAY

SWEDEN

FINLAND

ESTONIA

LATVIA

LITHUANIA

EAST PRUSSIA

USSR

North Sea

Baltic Sea

IRELAND

UNITED KINGDOM

DENMARK

POLAND

NETHER-LANDS

BELGIUM

GERMANY

CZECHOSLOVAKIA

FRANCE

SWITZER-LAND

AUSTRIA

HUNGARY

ROMANIA

Black Sea

YUGOSLAVIA

BULGARIA

TURKEY

PORTUGAL

SPAIN

Corsica

Sardinia

ITALY

ALBANIA

GREECE

Sicily

M e d i t e r r a n e a n   S e a

Caspi

SYRIA (French)

CYPRUS (British)

IRAQ (British)

PALESTINE (British)

TRANS-JORDAN (British)

TUNISIA (French)

ALGERIA (French)

Apr–Nov 1941

End Sept 1940

Feb 1941

LIBYA (Italian)

North Africa front lines

EGYPT (British)

HITLER'S TRIUMPHS

Throughout the period from September 1939 to the autumn of 1941, there was never a moment when an impartial observer would have bet on anyone apart from Germany winning the war. The parade of German military successes seemed endless, with Poland, Denmark and Norway, France and the Low Countries, the Balkans and, finally, most of European Russia coming under German domination. This rapid succession of victories had made Hitler's domestic position unassailable and convinced him of his own military genius, which would prove to be less infallible, however, in the years to come.

Remarkably, Britain was fighting on, with increasing help from the USA, but it was hard to see how anything Britain could do would really hurt Germany – nor did it seem likely that the Red Army could recover from the crushing defeats recently inflicted on it. Also, by late 1941, the brutal nature of the war had been made plain. Both the Nazis and the Soviets had murdered many thousands of Poles, and the Nazis had continued with mass killings of Jews and others on Soviet soil.

Yet the signs of a turning tide were there to be seen. America was rearming fast and inching closer to joining the war even before Japan's surprise attack on Pearl Harbor, while in that same week carefully husbanded Soviet reserves went into action on the Moscow front and threw back the German advance.

The USA and the European War President Roosevelt's "fireside chats" on the radio were famous.

The British Home Front Child evacuees leaving London in 1939 say goodbye to their parents.

The Fall of France A German Ju 87 Stuka bomber, one of the decisive weapons of Blitzkrieg.

Poland and the Outbreak of War

Bolstered by his pact with Stalin, Hitler no longer felt any need to restrain his aggression. Hitler first, and then Stalin, attacked and quickly conquered Poland while Britain and France did nothing other than declare war on Germany.

The first shots of the European half of WWII were fired at a Polish naval base by the old German coast-defence ship *Schleswig-Holstein* early in the morning of 1 September 1939. Already Hitler's Luftwaffe was screaming in to attack Polish air bases and German troops were surging over the borders. Britain and France responded by sending ultimata to Germany demanding an immediate withdrawal. When there was no response they declared war on the 3rd.

THE POLISH CAMPAIGN

Germany deployed 53 divisions for the attack, including all 6 Panzer (or armoured) divisions then in existence. The Army Commander-in-Chief, General Walther von Brauchitsch, controlled the operation with little interference from Hitler. Poland

Below: A Soviet tank passes a line of German troops in Brest-Litovsk, Poland, late September 1939.

KEY FACTS

PLACE: Poland

DATE: 1–28 September 1939

OUTCOME: Poland is attacked and completely overrun by Germany and then the USSR.

had not begun mobilizing its forces until 30 August, so many reservists were still on their way to their units. The Poles had about 23 divisions deployed, with very few tanks. However, they did have a significant cavalry force, though it is untrue (as sometimes has been suggested) that the cavalry were used to charge German tanks at various points in the fighting.

In the air German superiority was even more marked, with the Luftwaffe using about 1,600 modern aircraft against the Polish force of some 500 mostly obsolescent types.

With their superior strength, equipment and training the Germans soon gained the upper hand. Poland's Commander-in-Chief, Marshal Edward Smigly-Rydz, had decided to defend along the borders and his troops were soon thrown out of the exposed positions this plan committed them to. By the middle of the month the Polish forces had been split into isolated small groups, while the Germans were closing in on Warsaw – which they captured, ending the campaign on the 28th after a vicious artillery and air bombardment.

By then Stalin had taken his share of the spoils. Soviet troops crossed into Poland on the 17th, as agreed with Hitler in the Nazi–Soviet Pact; by the end of the month the Soviets had occupied about half the country. The official Soviet line was that

Below: German troops in Poland in September 1939. Few German units were motorized like this one.

GLEIWITZ

As a pretext to justify the attack on Poland, an SS unit faked an attack by Polish troops on a German radio station at Gleiwitz (Gliwice) in Silesia near the Polish border. The "attackers" captured the station late on 31 August, made a brief anti-German broadcast, then left after killing a concentration camp prisoner they had brought with them. This unfortunate person was then displayed to foreign pressmen as a civilian victim of Polish brutality.

Above: German troops crossing the San River in southern Poland, watched by their proud *Führer*.

they were intervening to protect the ethnic Belorussians and Ukrainians, but in fact they were annexing this territory. On the 29th the Germans and Soviets announced a friendship treaty that confirmed the partition of Poland.

THE PHONEY WAR

As well as Britain and France and their various colonies, who were given no choice in the matter, Britain's so-called "old dominions" declared war on Germany in the first days of September. Each, however, had some reservations.

For example, the Australian government declared war and introduced conscription, but only for home defence. Canada declared war only after this had been debated in parliament and also decided not to have conscription. The United States proclaimed its neutrality – there was no doubt at this stage that most Americans wanted to keep out of the war in Europe.

Although they had gone to war on Poland's behalf, Britain and France did nothing to help the Poles. For the moment Hitler was content not to provoke them further – German forces in the West in September were very weak. British government ministers refused to bomb industries in the Ruhr because the factories were private property, while French troops made only tentative forward moves in a small area of the Saar. This "Phoney War" would continue on the Western Front until Germany's attack in 1940.

Below: British families building Anderson shelters as a precaution against German air raids, during the Phoney War.

The Baltic and Scandinavia

Northern Europe's smaller nations continued to fall to aggression through 1939 and 1940. The USSR attacked Finland in November 1939 and annexed the Baltic States in 1940, while Norway and Denmark were taken by the Nazis that spring.

Stalin's plans for his Western neighbours were first demonstrated in the Soviet-occupied parts of Poland. By the end of October 1939 mass arrests and deportations of "enemies of socialism" had begun and fraudulent elections had appointed assemblies, which dutifully voted for incorporation into the USSR.

At the same time Lithuania, Latvia and Estonia were forced to conclude "friendship" agreements, giving the Soviets the right to station troops in these countries. In June 1940 Stalin activated these treaties and sent his troops in. The same process as in Poland quickly followed: terror, false elections and annexation by the USSR. In June 1940 the USSR annexed the Northern Bukovina and Bessarabia regions (formerly part of Romania) as well. They, too, had no option but to yield to Stalin's ultimatum.

Above: Finnish troops used their mastery of the winter conditions to defeat the initial Soviet attacks.

Below: A German tank and German infantry on the advance early in the Norwegian campaign.

THE WINTER WAR

These moves were part of a process of extending Soviet power and, at the same time, establishing a buffer zone against a possible German attack. Finland had been assigned to the Soviet sphere of interest by the Nazi–Soviet Pact and, in October 1939, Stalin began moves against the Finns.

He demanded that Finland cede territory in the Karelian Isthmus area in the south and in the far north, in return for land to be ceded to Finland in the central part of their border region. The Finns, fearing that this unusual generosity on Stalin's part was the thin end of a very nasty wedge, refused. On 30 November Stalin sent in the Red Army to attack Finland.

Right: A British anti-aircraft battery in Norway. The Germans had complete air superiority.

The Finns had 9 divisions facing 26 Soviet divisions, which also had massive superiority in air support, artillery, tanks and every other material category. Remarkably, the Finnish troops (well-trained and mobile on their skis) completely outfought the Soviets until early February 1940, when Soviet reinforcements under a new commander, Marshal Semyon Timoshenko, began wearing them down. An armistice came into effect on 13 March – the Finns conceded territory similar to that originally demanded.

The war had several repercussions. It was the final nail in the coffin of the League of Nations – the USSR was expelled but took no notice of this severe punishment. It also made clear the hesitancy of Britain and France, who considered the possibility of sending help to the Finns (even at the risk of war with the USSR) but did nothing until far too late.

Part of the reason for helping Finland was that, in crossing Norway to get there, the Anglo-French forces would also be able to interrupt Germany's iron-ore supplies from northern Sweden. The difficulty was that neither of these neutral countries wanted foreign troops on their territory. Finally, the war also highlighted what seemed to be the low quality of the Red Army – Hitler for one took note.

DENMARK AND NORWAY

In the aftermath of the Russo-Finnish War, Hitler became convinced (and correctly) that Britain and France still planned to intervene against his Swedish sources of iron ore by moving through Norway. On 9 April 1940 German forces advanced overland into Denmark and attacked a series of points along the Norwegian coast from the air and sea. Neither country had significant armed forces and the Western Allies were taken completely by surprise. Denmark was conquered within hours. Norway took about two months but the result was never really in doubt from the first days, when Germany established air bases in the country that more than compensated for Britain's superior naval strength.

Small Anglo-French forces arrived to help the Norwegians at various points, but the organization of these expeditions was chaotic. The last ones were withdrawn in early June, in the light of the disasters by then occurring on the Western Front.

Below: The German battle-cruiser *Scharnhorst* firing on the British carrier *Glorious* off Norway in June.

The Fall of France

The French Army was traditionally one of Europe's strongest, but in 1940 it was utterly defeated in a few weeks of combat. The disaster was caused by poor morale and weak leadership in the face of a ruthless and well-organized enemy.

Although there was no significant fighting on the Western Front before May 1940, many plans were made. Hitler intended to attack, and eventually he approved a radical plan to avoid becoming bogged down in assaults on France's Maginot Line defences. Instead, secondary forces were to advance into Belgium and the Netherlands, defeating these countries but, at the same time, drawing Anglo-French troops forward to help them. Then the main German force, led by most of the Panzer divisions, would advance through the Ardennes region (despite its unpromising terrain) and cut the Allied front in two.

Allied strategy was defensive, aiming to build strength while waiting for Britain's naval

BLITZKRIEG IN THE WEST
France, the Low Countries and the British expeditionary force were all defeated in less than six weeks.

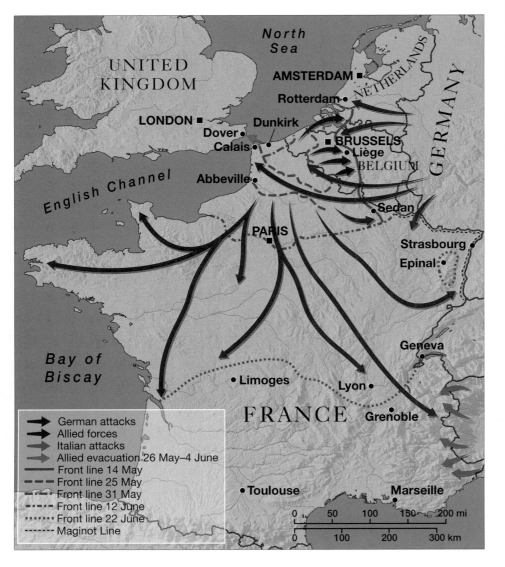

Above: A Ju 87 Stuka in its attack dive, a terrifying experience for those targeted on the ground below.

blockade of Germany to bite. Their plan, in the event of a German attack, was for the best Allied troops to advance into Belgium and link with both the Belgians and Dutch to present a united front. Unfortunately, in their understandable desperation to remain neutral and do nothing to provoke Hitler, the Belgians and Dutch refused to plan jointly with the Allies, so the whole scheme was never properly worked out.

BALANCE OF FORCES
Overall, counting the Dutch and Belgians, the two sides' land forces were roughly equal in May 1940, with some 140

divisions and 3,000 tanks each. However, most of the Allied armour was split up into small scattered groups, while Germany's was concentrated in well-trained Panzer divisions. In the air Germany deployed some 3,000 modern combat aircraft; the Allies had about 2,000, many of them older types. This would be a crucial advantage.

The German offensive began on 10 May. As the Germans had intended, attention was concentrated at first in the north. Within days a combination of heavy air attacks, paratroop operations and advances on the ground smashed the Dutch and Belgian forces. On 14 May the Netherlands surrendered. Britain and France played into German hands – the troops advancing into Belgium were reinforced but they were still unable to hold their positions against the German troops directly attacking them.

CROSSING THE MEUSE

In the meantime, the main German force had reached the River Meuse, crossed it on 14–15 May and was soon racing for the Channel. The Germans reached the coast on the 20th, slicing the Allied armies in two, just as they had planned. Unfortunately, the French Commander-in-Chief had kept no reserves to deal with any such emergency.

Over the next two weeks or so the Allied divisions in the north were forced back into an ever-smaller perimeter around the port of Dunkirk. About 340,000 troops were evacuated from there to Britain by 4 June, including some 120,000 French. The British had to leave all their

BLITZKRIEG

Germany's many successes in 1939–40 were ascribed to a new form of warfare, Blitzkrieg ("lightning war"), a term which is said to have been coined by Hitler himself. It described the combination of fast-moving tank forces and powerful close air support that overran France in a matter of weeks. Although it seemed to depend mainly on armoured units, the secret of Blitzkrieg was more to do with effective co-operation between all the arms of service. This, and the high levels of initiative shown by commanders at all levels, was the true basis of Germany's victories. The Germany Army would remain superior to all its enemies in these areas for most of the war.

equipment behind and many thousands more French troops were taken prisoner.

By then the Germans had regrouped and were ready to finish the job. On the 5th they attacked south from along the

Above: British soldiers crammed aboard a destroyer during the evacuation from Dunkirk.

line of the River Somme and were soon advancing speedily, despite some fierce initial resistance from the remaining French forces. They were in Paris on the 14th and, on the 16th, the French government resigned.

FRANCE SURRENDERS

The new government was headed by Marshal Philippe Pétain. Despite being urged to fight on by the British under their recently appointed Prime Minister, Winston Churchill, Pétain and his cabinet decided to ask for an armistice. France duly surrendered on 22 June.

Below: Panzer 1 light tanks seen during the French campaign. The less capable Panzer 1 and 2 designs were still a significant part of the German force in 1940.

The Battle of Britain and the Blitz

In the summer of 1940 Hitler seemed unbeatable, but his failure to finish Britain off can be seen as the point when the war changed from being a short one, which Germany would win, to a longer one which the Nazis could conceivably lose.

With France beaten and the British Army practically disarmed after the evacuation from Dunkirk, Hitler probably expected Britain to surrender. However, inspired by Churchill, Britain seemed ready to fight on. On 16 July Hitler therefore ordered his armed forces to start preparing for an invasion of England. Already the Luftwaffe had begun attacks on British shipping in the English Channel, in order to draw the Royal Air Force (RAF) into battle. Since Britain's Royal Navy was still very powerful and much of the German Navy had been lost during the Norwegian campaign, winning air superiority was an essential prelude to invasion.

Above: Firefighters at work on burning buildings in the City of London during the 1940 Blitz.

BRITAIN'S DEFENCES

Fortunately, Britain had made effective preparations. RAF Fighter Command had about 900 Spitfire and Hurricane aircraft, with plenty more being produced to replace the inevitable losses, but trained pilots were in much shorter supply. The defensive organization was excellent, with information from the radar system being fed to a network of control stations and then being used to direct the fighters into combat.

No other nation had such an integrated organization at this time. The Germans did not realize how well this system worked and, accordingly, would not make enough effort to disrupt it by attacks on the radar and control stations.

The Germans had a similar number of single-engined fighters (Messerschmitt Bf 109s) to the RAF, along with over 1,200 twin-engined medium bombers. In addition, they had twin-engined Messerschmitt 110 fighters and Junkers 87 Stuka dive-bombers, about 300 of each; both these types would prove less effective in this campaign than previously.

Whereas Britain was using a defensive system that had been in preparation for many months, Germany had to fight a new sort of battle, very different from their earlier campaigns in support of a land offensive. Their intelligence on RAF strength was very poor, so it was difficult to devise effective plans.

Left: Hawker Hurricane fighters of a squadron with refugee Czech pilots taking off in late 1940.

Right: A formation of Heinkel 111 bombers assembling for a raid during the Battle of Britain.

Above: Air Marshal Hugh Dowding, the successful Commander-in-Chief of RAF Fighter Command during the Battle of Britain.

All-out attacks began in mid-August 1940. There were heavy losses on both sides but the RAF had the advantage initially. Then, for a few days in late August and early September, the Luftwaffe changed its tactics and stepped up strikes against the front-line RAF airfields. This change stretched the RAF to the utmost but the German commanders did not realize that they were winning the battle.

On 7 September Germany switched tactics again and began a series of mass day and night attacks on London, which were heavily defeated on the 15th. On the 17th Hitler postponed his invasion plans. Daylight attacks and air battles continued for several weeks, but the Battle of Britain had been won.

THE BLITZ

London's ordeal was not over. The German bombers came back almost every night, up to 400 or more strong, until late November. By then they were also attacking a range of major cities that included Coventry, Birmingham and others. From November through to May 1941, when the attacks ended because most of the Luftwaffe was being transferred to eastern Europe, the main targets were various port areas like Merseyside and Clydeside. The British people called these attacks the "Blitz" (from the German word "Blitzkrieg").

At first the British defences were very ineffective. There were few anti-aircraft guns in service and radar-equipped night fighters were only just being developed. Although matters improved as the battle went on, the German loss rate remained low. Some 43,000 British civilians were killed and tens of thousands made homeless in the Blitz, but Britain's war effort was scarcely scratched.

The British Home Front

Although circumstances meant that British troops were never committed to the fight in numbers to match the 1914–18 war, the British people in WWII were more completely mobilized in support of the war effort than in any other country.

Although Britain was and remained a democratic society, governed with the consent of the people, life in Britain during WWII was in many ways as rigorously controlled as in the totalitarian nations. Britain also devoted its national resources more thoroughly to fighting the war than any other country, totalitarian or democratic.

Although in the end Britain was lightly bombed by comparison with the major Axis powers, fears of air attack had important effects from the first. Within weeks of the outbreak of war, over 800,000 unaccompanied children had been evacuated from major cities and billeted with families of strangers in

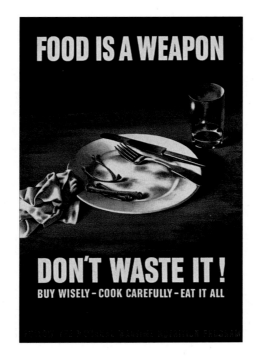

Above: Since much food was imported, reducing waste was vital.

safer areas of the countryside. Many returned home during the Phoney War only to be evacuated again in the Blitz, and repeat the process during the V-weapon attacks of 1944–5. In all some 6 million civilians, adults and children were involved.

AIR RAID PRECAUTIONS

Various Civil Defence services, including Air Raid Wardens, were organized with hundreds of thousands of members. Public air raid shelters were built or dug in parks; when the sirens sounded Londoners took to the tunnels of the Tube; and 1.5 million householders installed free family refuges called Anderson Shelters. Everyone implemented the blackout at night; it may have done little to misdirect enemy bombers but certainly caused a great increase in road accidents.

Many of the innovations of the war followed from the Emergency Powers Act, which was passed by parliament in May 1940. This act gave the government dictatorial authority over every aspect of life, and it was used extensively. As well as men conscripted into the forces, for example, the government could direct civilian men and women into particular jobs, control their wages in those jobs and forbid them to leave.

Left: Children being evacuated from London in 1939 say their goodbyes to their mothers.

Above: The number of British women working in agriculture more than tripled during the war.

When he took over as Prime Minister in May 1940 and transformed the country's previously lethargic war effort, Churchill formed a coalition government including Labour and Liberal members but principally drawn from his own Conservative Party. Its methods, however, were distinctly socialist in nature, with centralized planning of manpower, food, fuel, the economy and much more. The government was involved in almost every aspect of daily life. The civil service had to double in size to control it all.

Rationing of food, fuel, clothing and other goods was one of the most pervasive effects of the war. Petrol rationing was introduced in the first months of the war, with meat, butter and sugar added in 1940. Staple foods like bread and potatoes were never rationed – and the "Dig for Victory" campaign encouraged people to grow their own food. Factory canteens,

relatively unusual until the war, also supplied many decent meals. Naturally, a black market did develop, but generally speaking the system worked well and was seen to be fair. It was also undoubtedly true that the poorest people, often unemployed and undernourished in the pre-war years, were much better fed during wartime.

THE BEVERIDGE REPORT

Planning for a better future was a major theme even when a successful outcome for the war was still uncertain. The Beveridge Report of December 1942 proposed schemes of "social insurance" to combat unemployment and provide health care. These and other developments would be embodied in what came to be described as the welfare state after WWII.

All in all, people in 1945 felt that their country had behaved well. They had stood up to Hitler from the first and had fought in a united and purposeful manner. They had high hopes for the future, not all of which would be fulfilled.

WINSTON CHURCHILL

Churchill (1874–1965) was Britain's Prime Minister from May 1940 until after the end of the war in Europe. He became a government minister in September 1939, after a long period in the political wilderness, because he had been among the first to see the true nature of the menace facing Britain. This and his natural pugnacity won him the premiership the next May. His inspirational leadership would keep Britain fighting over the coming months. At the same time he worked ceaselessly to bring the USA into the war, recognizing far better than anyone else that this alone would bring victory. It is no exaggeration to say that Europe would have entirely fallen to the Nazis without Churchill's courage.

Above: Prime Minister Churchill in a characteristic pose.

Left: Bevin Boys were young men conscripted to work in the coal mines because of the labour shortage later in the war.

The Battle of the Atlantic, 1939–41

U-boats and Allied anti-submarine forces were in action from the first day of the war to the last. The Battle of the Atlantic was the longest campaign of the war and if Hitler had won it he would almost certainly have won the war, too.

Britain imported roughly half its food, all its oil and many other items essential to the war economy. In addition British forces and the supplies they needed had to be shipped overseas if Britain was to fight its enemies. Since this traffic had to sail to and from British ports, the Atlantic accordingly became a major theatre of war.

THE GERMAN THREAT

Germany's Kriegsmarine was poorly prepared for war in 1939, with few powerful surface ships and a small force of submarines. Only from the spring of 1941

Above: Günther Prien, one of the top U-boat commanders of 1940–1. Prien sank HMS *Royal Oak* in 1939.

would German U-boat strength increase substantially. For the first year or so of the war about a third of German torpedoes failed to explode, which obviously thwarted many attacks.

Drawing on the lessons of WWI, Britain had planned a convoy system to protect its merchantmen, but there were so few escort ships in service initially that this could only be applied to the few hundred kilometres of their journeys nearest the British Isles. Although the escorts did have asdic (later called sonar) for finding a submerged submarine, they did not at first have radar or effective tactics for convoy protection. Britain had few aircraft committed to maritime duties and, until many months into the war, these also did not have radar to find a submarine on the

Raid by *Scharnhorst* & *Gneisenau* Jan–Mar 1941
Raid by *Bismarck* May 1941
Bismarck chase ••••••• Aircraft carrier attacks
✕ Major battles

Above: *U-570* in a British port after surrendering to a British aircraft following damage in an air attack.

MAJOR SURFACE ACTIONS OF THE EUROPEAN WAR

The Royal Navy won most battles against the Germans and Italians.

surface nor weapons likely to damage a U-boat that had dived. However, although the German surface and U-boat forces achieved successes up to June 1940, these were not significant enough to pose a real problem.

"THE HAPPY TIME"

The fall of France in 1940 brought a major change. Within hours of the surrender the head of the U-boat force, Admiral Karl Dönitz, had equipment trains rolling to France's Atlantic ports, hundreds of kilometres nearer the convoy routes than previous German bases. What the U-boat crews called the "Happy Time" was about to begin. Until the spring of 1941 a series of U-boat commanders became celebrated as "aces", sinking ship after ship with little loss on the German side.

They used so-called "wolf-pack" tactics whereby the first boat to sight a convoy signalled U-boat headquarters, which then manoeuvred a group into attack positions. Then, at night, the U-boats would sail on the surface right in among the convoy's ships – without radar it was almost impossible to spot a surfaced U-boat. The U-boats would tor-

pedo perhaps several ships and escape into the dark amid the resulting carnage. In this period the Germans also had the upper hand in the code-breaking struggle. Their messages remained secure, but many British ones giving away convoy routes and other movements did not.

Things improved for the Allies in the spring of 1941. Britain began breaking the U-boat codes. Escort ship numbers increased so that convoys could be protected all the way across the Atlantic. The escorts and their few supporting aircraft began to be fitted with effective radar sets. And the USA started taking a more active role, even though still officially neutral.

Above: The German battleship *Bismarck* after sinking HMS *Hood* in May 1941. *Bismarck* is down by the bow because of battle damage.

In April 1941 President Roosevelt extended the Pan-American Neutrality Zone and in July US Marines occupied Iceland. Ships of any nationality travelling between there and the USA were protected by the US Navy. By the autumn the Americans were effectively fighting alongside the British and the much-expanded Royal Canadian Navy. Although Allied shipping losses therefore declined sharply in the second half of 1941, the struggle was clearly by no means over.

SURFACE RAIDERS

The Kriegsmarine also used warships and disguised armed merchant ships in raids on Allied trade routes. Germany's three "pocket battleships" made various generally unsuccessful voyages and one, *Graf Spee*, was sunk in December 1939. The more powerful *Scharnhorst* and *Gneisenau* made a more worthwhile sortie in early 1941. The still bigger *Bismarck* sank HMS *Hood* on 24 May 1941 but was itself hunted down three days later. Seven disguised raiders made a number of voyages during 1940–1 and proved very difficult to track down, operating successfully for extended periods in the Pacific and Indian Oceans as well as the South Atlantic.

Above: A well-ordered convoy is seen from an American patrol aircraft shortly after leaving port.

The Mediterranean Theatre, 1940–1

*Thrown out of mainland Europe at Dunkirk, Britain concentrated on the
Mediterranean and attacks on Germany's ally Italy in the early-war years.
Mussolini's declaration of war in June 1940 would soon seem unwise.*

As France was crashing to defeat in June 1940, Mussolini declared war on the Allies, determined not to miss out on a share of the spoils. Italy had annexed Albania without a fight in the spring of 1939 (this had been recognized by Britain as part of the then still current appeasement process). Then, in the summer of 1940, Mussolini picked a quarrel with Greece, which had been trying desperately to stay out of the war. On 28 October Italian troops crossed the border from Albania but their advance into Greece was soon halted and turned back by the Greek forces. By March 1941 half of Albania was under Greek control.

Italy also had large armies in its North African colony of Libya, as well as in East Africa in Italian Somaliland and

Above: Guns and crew of a British A9 cruiser tank in Egypt, May 1940.

Abyssinia. In August 1940 troops from Abyssinia occupied British and French Somaliland. Then, in September, the Italian Tenth Army crossed from Libya into Egypt but it halted and dug in after a short distance.

In all these campaigns the weakness of the Italian forces was apparent. The troops were generally ill-trained and badly

led and had little commitment to the fight. Equipment on land, at sea and in the air had many shortcomings, with flimsy tanks, outmoded biplane aircraft, inaccurate naval guns and more. Results soon made this plain.

ITALIAN DISASTERS

The most spectacular Italian defeat was in the North African desert. By December 1940 the British force in Egypt was ready to respond to the initial Italian advance. Within two months the Italian Tenth Army had been thrown back to El Agheila (Al-'Uqaylah) and lost 130,000 prisoners at a cost of only 550 British dead. However, the

NORTH AFRICA, 1940–2
The Desert War saw a remarkable sequence of changing fortunes, with first one side, then the other on top.

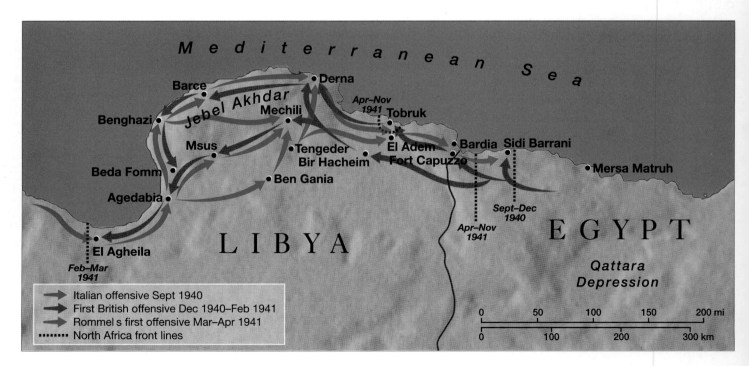

Italian offensive Sept 1940
First British offensive Dec 1940–Feb 1941
Rommel's first offensive Mar–Apr 1941
North Africa front lines

British position was becoming less secure. Troops had already been withdrawn to East Africa; others would soon go to Greece.

ENTER ROMMEL

Embarrassed by his Italian ally's failures, Hitler sent an ambitious young general called Erwin Rommel to Libya in February 1941 with a small force to block any further British advance.

Rommel spotted how weak the British front had become and attacked at the end of March. Within a month the British had been pushed all the way back into Egypt, with their worn-out tanks falling easy victims to the superior German equipment and tactics. Two minor British offensives – at the end of April and again in June – also failed after several further demonstrations of the superior German fighting skills.

Fortunately for the Allied side, one of their campaigns had a much greater success. During January and February 1941 the British, Indian and African troops that had been based in Sudan and Kenya went on the attack into Abyssinia and Italian Somaliland. Most of the Italian troops had been defeated by May though the final surrender did not come until November.

At sea Britain's morale was boosted by substantial gains over the powerful Italian fleet. Early skirmishes went Britain's way. On 11 November 1940, a night air attack by carrier planes on the Italian base at Taranto crippled three battleships.

Right: Some of the tens of thousands of Italian prisoners who were captured by the British in Libya in December 1940.

British forces based on Malta were then able to step up their attacks on the supply routes between Italy and North Africa, contributing greatly to the British success in the desert. In turn, when German air forces arrived in Sicily in strength in early 1941, this helped the land battle swing Rommel's way.

In March 1941 the Battle of Matapan confirmed the weakness of the Italian fleet. Three

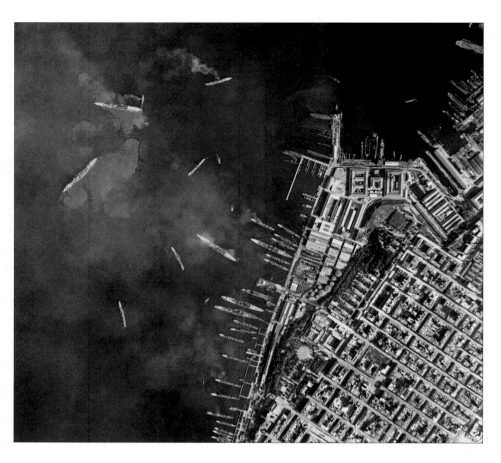

Above: Damaged ships in Taranto Harbour, here seen in a British photograph taken after the attack.

Italian heavy cruisers were caught and sunk while on the retreat from Admiral Andrew Cunningham's Mediterranean Fleet. Even though British naval strength declined substantially in the following months, the Italians would not make a major challenge at sea again.

The Balkans and North Africa, 1941–2

In 1941 Hitler established what looked like a secure grip on the Balkan region, protecting his southern flank for the attack on the USSR. Changing fortunes in North Africa brought the British back to a desperate defence of Egypt in mid-1942.

Hitler's main plan for 1941 was to attack the USSR, but he also wanted to secure German control over south-eastern Europe. In the winter of 1940–1 Hungary, Romania and Bulgaria all in effect allied themselves with Germany. Greece, however, was winning its war with Italy in Albania and was receiving increasing help from Britain. This brought the unwelcome prospect of British aircraft based in Greece within relatively easy striking distance of the Romanian oilfields on which Germany greatly relied.

From late 1940, the Germans therefore prepared an attack on Greece. In late March 1941 when it seemed that the Yugoslavian government, after much pressure, was going to join the German bloc, a military coup reversed the situation and a furious Hitler ordered an immediate German attack.

The Germans deployed overwhelming forces for their offensive both in the air and on

Below: A German transport plane crashes over Suda Bay during the invasion of Crete in May 1941.

Above: German troops in northern Yugoslavia during the rapid and successful invasion of April 1941.

the ground. The strike against Yugoslavia started with heavy air raids on Belgrade on 6 April. The main land advance began from Romania on the 8th and was joined in succeeding days by converging attacks from both Hungary and Austria. There was little resistance and the Yugoslavs agreed an armistice on the 17th. German casualties for the campaign were fewer than 200 dead.

By 6 April 1941 three British Empire divisions and supporting forces had been sent to Greece, substantially weakening the British position in North

Africa. However, with much of the Greek Army already committed to the Albanian front and the remainder poorly deployed, there was little chance of the combination resisting the Germans for long. By the end of April the whole of mainland Greece had been overrun. The last act of the campaign was the capture of Crete by German airborne forces on 20–31 May.

DESERT BATTLES

After their defeats in the first half of 1941, it took until November for the British forces in North Africa to prepare a new offensive. They started their advance across the border from Egypt into Libya on the 18th.

A bewildering series of manoeuvres and tank battles followed over the next three weeks or so. Much of the Allied superiority in numbers was frittered away by poor command, but eventually the exhausted German forces and their Italian allies had to retreat. As before this meant retiring all the way to El Agheila on the Gulf of Sirte, which Rommel reached at the end of December.

However, the pendulum was set to swing once more. German air strength in the Mediterranean was increased again and British naval power was at a low ebb, while Rommel's supply situation quickly improved. On land much British strength had been dissipated and resources and troops that might have come

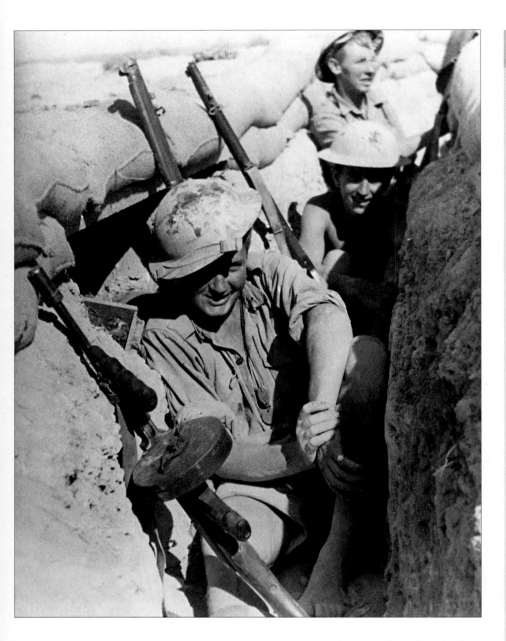

Above: Australian troops like these made up a large part of Tobruk's garrison during the siege in 1941.

to North Africa were instead being sent to face the Japanese advance in the Pacific. Less than a month after ending his retreat, Rommel attacked again.

NEW GERMAN ADVANCE

In the first stage, completed by early February 1942, the British were pushed out of most of the territory they had just captured. Next, in a three-week battle from 26 May, British defences on the so-called Gazala Line were overcome, despite being held by superior forces. Tobruk (Tubruq), which had survived a long siege after Rommel's first advance, was quickly captured this time with a great mass of supplies, which helped support Rommel's *Afrika Korps* for a charge into Egypt. After a disordered and panicky retreat, the British made a stand near an obscure railway halt called El Alamein in the first days of July. Rommel's last desperate attacks were fought to a standstill in the First Battle of El Alamein. Now both sides would settle down to rebuild their worn-out forces.

ERWIN ROMMEL

Field Marshal Rommel (1891–1944) became famous as Germany's commander in North Africa during 1941-2. Rommel took his first steps to fame when he was given command of a Panzer division in 1940. In 1941 he was appointed to lead German troops in Africa, which he did with considerable skill until outmatched by greater Allied resources in the late summer of 1942. In 1944 he commanded the troops opposing the D-Day landings but was wounded in an Allied air attack shortly after. He was forced to commit suicide later in the year because he had been implicated in the Bomb Plot against Hitler.

Above: Rommel (nearest) and Marshal Italo Gariboldi, the commander of the Italian forces in North Africa in 1941.

The USA and the European War

For over two years after Hitler attacked Poland the USA remained neutral, though all the time it sent increasing help to Britain and the other Allies. Even so it took Hitler's declaration of war to confirm that the USA would fight Germany.

Since the end of WWI the United States had returned to its traditional foreign policy of keeping out of overseas conflicts and maintaining only modest armed forces. By September 1939 this "isolationism" had been backed by strict neutrality laws that prevented the US government or private corporations from selling arms or giving loans to countries at war. Most Americans blamed Germany for starting the war and hoped that Britain and France would win it, but they were also very clear that the USA should stay out.

President Roosevelt and his government saw things a little differently. They recognized the evil of the Nazi regime, and of Japan's militarism, and that (as well as being morally repugnant)

Below: In September 1940 in the "destroyers for bases" deal, Britain was given old US Navy ships like these to fight the U-boat menace.

Above: Pioneer aviator Charles Lindbergh, one of the leaders of the isolationist America First movement.

they presented a real threat to the USA's interests. Roosevelt no more wanted war than did the American people so his policy was to help the European Allies with "all means short of war", while being as tough with the Japanese as possible without provoking them to attack. The

details of this changed over time but the general principles held good up to December 1941.

NOT QUITE NEUTRAL

The first step came in November 1939 when the "cash and carry" law was passed. Countries at war could buy American arms with cash (not on credit), provided they transported them overseas on their own ships. The facts of geography and Britain's large navy meant that this would only benefit the Allies, as was intended.

The hope that this would be enough to ensure an Anglo-French victory fell apart with France's surrender in June 1940. The USA's rearmament was immediately stepped up, in particular by the Two-Ocean Navy

Below: Roosevelt took leading Republicans into his cabinet, including Frank Knox, here being sworn in as Navy Secretary.

FRANKLIN D. ROOSEVELT

Roosevelt (1882–1945) was President of the USA from 1933 to his death. While Churchill's wartime leadership is almost universally admired, Roosevelt's has always been more controversial. Although he was no warmonger, he saw clearly the threats posed by Germany and Japan and worked steadily to oppose them. Opponents, however, said that he deceived the American people over just how far he was going. He has also been criticized as being naive in his dealings with Stalin and the Chinese Nationalists. On the other hand his generous instincts were shown in his Lend-Lease policy, without which Britain and other Allies could not have continued the fight.

Right: Roosevelt giving one of his famed "fireside chat" radio broadcasts.

Act of July, which provided for a massive increase in American naval forces. This was designed to protect against the German threat but it also worried Japan. It would take a couple of years to build the ships but by then the Japanese would be unable to compete, unless they did something about it first.

Next, in the autumn of 1940, came the Selective Service Act, establishing conscription for the first time in US history when the nation was not at war.

LEND-LEASE

Roosevelt also continued to help Britain, although this carried risks – sending arms to Britain might mean Hitler getting them for free if he won the war. However, there was a new problem – Britain was about to run out of cash and would probably be unable to continue the war at all, never mind pay for more American goods. The answer was the "Lend-Lease" programme, in operation from March 1941. Britain, and later other Allies including the USSR, would be sent vast supplies of arms and other goods, produced initially at American expense, on the basis that they would be paid for or returned after the war.

Roosevelt was well aware that there was no point making arms for Britain only for the Germans to sink them on their way across the Atlantic. Through 1941, therefore, the US Navy played a more active part against Germany's U-boats in the Atlantic, though how far this was going was not made clear to the American people. By autumn US warships in the western Atlantic were doing the same things as the British and Canadians. It was equally clear, though, that Americans still wanted to avoid war. In August 1941 the Selective Service Act was only renewed in Congress by a single vote.

Throughout all this Hitler had been cautious, content to fight only the enemies he already had. Incomprehensibly, four days after Pearl Harbor, he changed his mind and declared war on the USA, a decision that doomed his regime to a defeat as crushing as that awaiting Japan.

Below: Men register for the draft in October 1940, under the terms of the new Selective Service Act.

German Rule in Europe

Life in the countries occupied by the Nazis was exceedingly harsh. Starvation rations, slave labour and other cruelties were everyday realities in all the occupied territories, though Jews and resisters fared worse still.

Racism was the whole basis of Germany's rule in Europe. Everything was to be done and organized for the benefit of both Germany and the *Volk* – the German race, as defined by Hitler and the Nazis. Within this system there were gradations. At the top were those like the Dutch or Norwegians, who were certainly regarded as second-class citizens but still worthy of some respect, and near the bottom were the Slavs, whose lives were valueless even if sometimes their labour was not. Jews were the lowest category of all.

The way in which conquered territories were ruled naturally varied within this hierarchy. In Poland or the Ukraine Nazi cruelty, organized and led by the SS, was open and extreme.

Above: A German officer and a British bobby in the Channel Islands, the only occupied British territory.

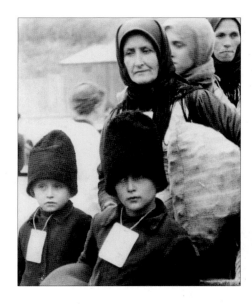

Above: *Volksdeutsche* from Bessarabia in Romania, on their way to be resettled in Germany.

Near the other end of the scale were countries like Norway, where local Nazi sympathizers were allowed the appearance of a say in the government. (Norway's Vidkun Quisling has given the English language a word for just this sort of traitor and was executed for his treason after the war.) Finally, there were nations like France where a government at least not hostile to Germany was allowed to control all or part of the country.

The "independence" of Marshal Pétain's Vichy regime was bought at a price, however. More than half of government revenue went straight to Germany to pay for the costs of the occupation forces and almost half of French industrial output was for German benefit. The franc was artificially valued, so that anything the Germans did pay for was acquired on unfair terms.

Food rationing was severe with the official provision set at an inadequate 1,200 calories per day, though many of the poorest did not even manage this – much food was diverted to an expensive black market. The experience of other Western European countries was similar in many of these respects.

FORCED LABOUR

As the war proceeded Germany became increasingly dependent on foreign labour to keep its economy running. This included around 1.5 million prisoners of war and, by 1943–4, some 5 million civilians, most of whom had been forced to work in Germany and many of whom were treated as slaves. Roughly a quarter of the workforce in Germany in the later war years was made up of foreigners.

The process started in 1939–40 when many Poles were brought to Germany as farm labourers. Later, in eastern Europe, men, women and many young children were simply rounded up and sent wherever it suited Germany. In Vichy France men were conscripted to do their national service in the German labour force.

VOLKSDEUTSCHE

People of German descent (known to the Nazis as *Volksdeutsche*) were living in many

Above: German officers enjoy a Paris café in the gentler early days of the occupation in 1940.

places in eastern Europe; one of the most bizarre aspects of Nazi rule was the plan to reassimilate them with the *Volk*. Hundreds of thousands of people were to be brought back into the Reich. Many were transported from their homes in the Baltic States or western USSR, supposedly to be resettled in captured territories that were to become part of Germany proper. Most ended up among the millions of homeless displaced persons in central Europe after the war.

Perhaps the most heartless aspect of this particular policy was the *Lebensborn* programme. As part of this plan to increase the German race, SS representatives toured occupied territories identifying "racially worthwhile" children and taking them for forced adoption in Germany. Some 300,000 children are believed to have been abducted from their families in this way; 80 per cent of them never returned.

HEINRICH HIMMLER

Himmler (1900–45) was head of the Nazi SS from 1929 to the fall of Hitler's regime. He built the SS up from being a relatively minor Nazi Party organization to a state within the state. He was in charge of Germany's whole police and security apparatus, of the party's murderous "racial policy" and of the German Army's rival, the Waffen-SS. Although he was personally responsible for numerous hideous cruelties, he was also a rather timid personality. He was captured by British forces at the end of the war and poisoned himself when his disguise as a private soldier was exposed.

Above: Reichsführer-SS Heinrich Himmler on parade.

Left: Hitler with his fervent admirer Vidkun Quisling. The Germans never gave Quisling any real power in occupied Norway.

Operation Barbarossa

Germany's invasion of the Soviet Union was the greatest military operation ever seen. Its outcome would decide the result of the war and the campaign would be fought on both sides with a vicious barbarity unequalled elsewhere.

Hitler had first ordered his generals to begin planning an attack on the Soviet Union even before the Battle of Britain was fought. Ultimately, the Nazis intended to occupy the whole of the European USSR, exterminating all Jews and communists and enslaving any surviving "sub-human" Slavs.

Although the Germans deployed a truly massive force of around 3 million men, 3,300 tanks and 2,700 aircraft, the task facing them was huge. They were outnumbered by the Red Army forces in the western USSR, and they greatly underestimated the size of the Soviet reserves in the Far East and elsewhere. They thought little of Soviet weapons or efficiency; indeed, only a quarter of the total 24,000-strong Soviet tank force was in running order – and German intelligence knew little of the superior Soviet weapons like the KV-1 and T-34 tanks, which were coming into service.

GERMANY'S PROBLEMS
The huge distances were daunting. The Germans had pressed hundreds of vehicles from every conquered nation into service but still needed over 600,000 horses for their transport needs. Most ordinary soldiers simply had to march. Roads everywhere were unmade or in dreadful condition, and the Soviet rail system ran on a different gauge, so the track would need to be converted before it could be used. The

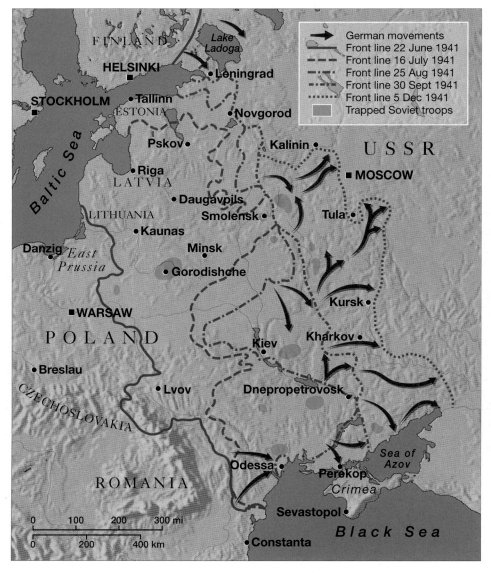

**Legend (map):**
- German movements
- Front line 22 June 1941
- Front line 16 July 1941
- Front line 25 Aug 1941
- Front line 30 Sept 1941
- Front line 5 Dec 1941
- Trapped Soviet troops

Below: Soviet troops fought with undoubted bravery in what they soon called the Great Patriotic War.

OPERATION BARBAROSSA
Neither Hitler nor his generals could decide which of their three main advances should have priority.

Above: Muddy roads across the endless steppe, with Panzers at war in the east in 1941.

problems in these areas would escalate the farther the advance went and as the bad weather of autumn and winter set in.

The Germans' greatest asset was that, despite many warnings, Stalin refused to allow proper preparations to be made and no one dared to argue. Why this was is a mystery. He seems to have been so frightened by the chance of a German attack that he tried everything he could to avoid provoking one.

THE BATTLE BEGINS

The German attack, Operation Barbarossa, began early on the morning of 22 June 1941. Within hours the leading tank forces had penetrated tens of kilometres into the unprepared Soviet defences and over a thousand Soviet aircraft were wrecked on their airfields. Within a week the two Panzer groups leading Army Group Centre's advance had completed a vast encirclement west of Minsk; 300,000 Red Army troops surrendered there by early July. In the meantime the attack had surged on toward Smolensk, another 320km (200 miles) nearer Moscow.

Progress on the other main attack front was also excellent; Army Group North had over-run the Baltic States and was closing in on Leningrad. The less powerful Army Group South, however, was being held up by Soviet resistance just west of Kiev. Neither Hitler nor his generals had been sure about the best strategy for the campaign from the start and now Hitler ordered a change of plan. Guderian's Second Panzer Group was to attack south, to help complete the capture of Kiev and not, as Guderian and other generals urged, immediately continue east to Moscow.

The results seemed to justify the decision. Over half a million Red Army troops were captured east of Kiev by mid-September. The ever wearier German troops redeployed to the Moscow front by the end of the month for what they hoped would be the final decisive attack.

However, the delay had brought the start of bad weather. After yet more fierce fighting, they reached Moscow's outer suburbs in early December but they could go no further. The German units were now a fraction of their former strength and the troops were suffering

General Guderian (1888–1954) was the man most responsible for the creation of the German Army's formidable Panzer arm. His pre-war book *Achtung! Panzer!* explained how tanks might be used in a new fast-moving style of war. He was highly successful in command of a Panzer corps in both Poland and France in 1939–40. These successes were repeated during the early months of Operation Barbarossa, but he was dismissed by Hitler that winter. He served in staff positions later in the war, but by then Hitler was making most of the decisions and Guderian's advice was seldom followed.

Above: General Guderian with his *Panzergruppe* in 1940.

horribly from the freezing weather. A quick victory had once seemed so certain that no supplies of winter clothing had been prepared. Instead a long, horrible struggle on the Eastern Front was now inevitable.

Horrors of War: The Eastern Front

The war on the Eastern Front was conducted with a savageness hardly seen elsewhere during WWII. The Nazis saw their enemies as valueless racial inferiors and to the Soviet leaders life was cheap – their own citizens' or anyone else's.

As the German drive on Moscow ground to a halt in temperatures of minus 40 or worse in early December 1941, the pitiless pattern of the war on the Eastern Front was already all too well established. Millions of civilians and prisoners of war (POW) would die near the front and behind the lines as a consequence of the fighting.

MASS MURDER

Before Operation Barbarossa began Hitler had ordered that any captured communist officials were to be killed. As it had done during the invasion of Poland, the SS formed *Einsatzgruppen* to follow behind the advancing armies. These murder squads (about 3,000 strong) had orders to eliminate all Jews and communists. By the end of 1941, as their own

Below: A German soldier gives himself up, winter 1941–2. Many German POWs died of ill treatment.

Above: A Red Army anti-tank gun crew advancing any way they can during the Battle for Moscow.

records attest, these squads had killed over 600,000 Jews in the occupied USSR.

POW on both sides also faced a grim fate. Over 5 million Red Army soldiers were taken prisoner by the Germans during the war, 3.8 million of them in 1941; only around 35 per cent of these survived their captivity. Prisoners on both sides were given little food. The only medical attention they received was from their own captured medical staff and any supplies they had.

It is likely that some of this maltreatment arose from lack of resources and incompetence, but the racism at the heart of Nazi ideology and the total disregard for human life central to Stalinism played a larger part. And, of course, many more who tried to surrender were simply shot out of hand. The Waffen-SS (a substantial portion of the German forces later in the war)

almost never took prisoners on the Eastern Front. The Soviet attitude to POW and potential enemies was clearly shown by their murder at Katyń and elsewhere of some 15,000 Polish Army officers who fell into their hands in 1939.

Around a fifth of the population of the German-occupied territories either fled as refugees or were evacuated by the Soviet authorities. Many were sent to work in the new factories being set up east of the Urals, where living and working conditions were harsh in the extreme. Significant numbers of those who remained behind might well have welcomed the Germans had they been well treated. Instead their lives and property were always at risk –

Right: An exhausted German soldier asleep in his muddy trench on the Eastern Front in early 1942.

whole villages were routinely burnt to the ground in retaliation for partisan activities. On the other hand partisans were often unpopular with civilians; they were tightly controlled by the communist hierarchy and quick to "discipline" those who failed to follow their lead.

MOSCOW ATTACK

Some of the most pitiless fighting of the campaign took place in the winter of 1941–2. On 6 December the Soviet forces began a successful counter-attack on the Moscow front, using fresh reserve forces assembled from the Far East. Unlike the Germans, the Soviet troops had good winter clothing and equipment fit to withstand the country's extreme cold.

Hitler's response was to order "fanatical resistance" and no retreat. It is possible that his order to stand fast was correct in this case and saved his forces from disintegration, but various of his best generals disagreed and were dismissed. Hitler took over himself as Commander-in-Chief of the Army and would now personally control all major military decisions on the Eastern Front. Although in places they were pushed back some 160km (100 miles), early 1942 saw the Germans solidifying their front line until all operations were halted as usual in the east by the spring thaw.

Below: Mass graves of some of the Polish officers murdered at Katyń.

Below: German soldiers beating a Russian villager as others watch.

Battleships and Battle-cruisers The USS *Indiana* shelling the Japanese coast in 1945.

Coral Sea and Midway Aircraft aboard the carrier USS *Enterprise* during the Battle of Midway.

Japan's Continuing Successes Burmese civilians look on as Japanese invaders pass by.

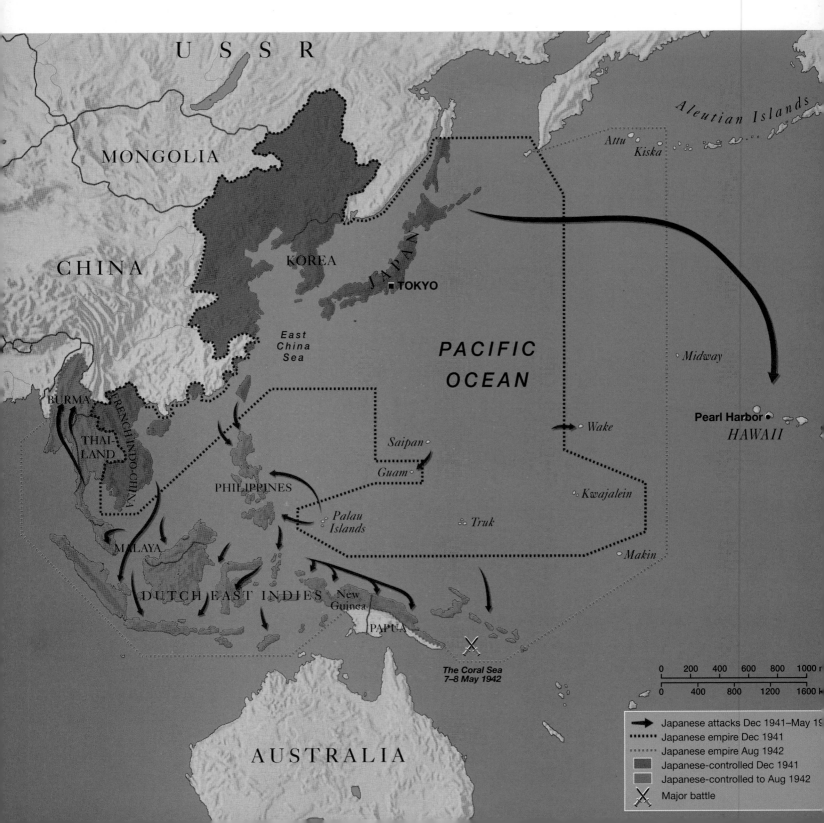

U S S R

MONGOLIA

CHINA

KOREA

JAPAN

TOKYO

East China Sea

PACIFIC OCEAN

Aleutian Islands

Attu
Kiska

Midway

Wake

Pearl Harbor
HAWAII

Saipan

Guam

Kwajalein

Truk

Makin

BURMA

THAI-LAND

FRENCH INDO-CHINA

PHILIPPINES

Palau Islands

MALAYA

DUTCH EAST INDIES

New Guinea

PAPUA

The Coral Sea 7–8 May 1942

AUSTRALIA

| 0 | 200 | 400 | 600 | 800 | 1000 r |
| 0 | 400 | 800 | 1200 | 1600 k |

→ Japanese attacks Dec 1941–May 19
····· Japanese empire Dec 1941
····· Japanese empire Aug 1942
▬ Japanese-controlled Dec 1941
▬ Japanese-controlled to Aug 1942
✕ Major battle

JAPAN'S PACIFIC CONQUESTS

Japan's attack on Pearl Harbor began a stunning half year of military triumphs that saw the overrunning of many British, American, French and Dutch colonies – from Burma in the west to a range of Pacific islands in the east and south. As well as the victories on land and the decimation of the US Pacific Fleet, British and other naval forces were practically wiped out throughout the theatre of operations and Allied air power was largely neutralized.

Japanese leaders had hoped that the conquest of these territories would give access to the natural resources their country desperately wanted and create a defensive perimeter that could be defended successfully against the worst their enemies might do. Instead, just as in their earlier and ongoing involvement in China, they were sucked into yet more advances, which confirmed what the most sensible Japanese commanders had long realized: in attacking the USA, as previously in China, they had bitten off far more than they could chew.

Japan also made much of plans for a Greater East Asia Co-Prosperity Sphere, a vague anti-imperialist alliance from which all native Asians might hope to benefit. In fact the expanded Japanese Empire created in 1941–2 turned out to be brutal, racist and exploitative.

The USA at War Making aircraft engines was a new area of work for American women.

Japan's Brutal Empire A sick British ex-prisoner gets medical treatment after his liberation in 1945.

Japan's First Advances General Percival signs the surrender of Singapore on 15 February 1942.

Approach to War in the Pacific

Throughout 1939–41 tension between Japan and the United States grew. Its armies increasingly bogged down in China, Japan decided to look south for the natural resources and the empire its leaders thought their country needed and deserved.

In early 1939 Japan's leaders were unsure what strategy to adopt to overcome their difficulties in China and their related economic problems. Some wished to attack north against the USSR, others to move south towards the European colonies of South-east Asia, with their substantial natural resources of oil, tin, rubber and much more.

VITAL SOVIET VICTORY

Japan had a long-standing enmity with Russia. Through the 1930s there had been frequent battles along the frontier between Japanese-controlled territory in north-east China and the Far Eastern provinces of the USSR. In the summer of 1939 there was particularly fierce fighting in the Khalkhin Gol region on the border between Soviet-backed Mongolia and China – and the Japanese were badly defeated.

These little-known battles were a decisive turning point in history. Both the Japanese Army and the government began looking more urgently at expanding to the south. In April 1941 Japan negotiated a Neutrality Agreement with the

Left: US Secretary of State Cordell Hull with Japan's Ambassador Nomura during the final pre-war negotiations in 1941.

Soviets and would stick to this decision, even when tempted to change it by Hitler's attack on the USSR in June 1941.

Tension between Japan and the USA and European colonial powers over events in China had grown in the 1930s. Japan was convinced that supplies reaching China through Burma and French Indo-China were vital in keeping the Chinese fighting. Then, in the summer of 1940, new possibilities opened up. Hitler's victories left the French and Dutch colonies virtually defenceless and British power in Asia gravely weakened while the USA's rearmament still had a long way to go.

In July 1940 the Japanese government formally decided on a twin policy: first, to win their existing war by blocking the supply routes to the Chinese; and second, to gain access to the desired raw materials from Malaysia and the East Indies, if necessary by a new war. This was the moment when war between Japan and the USA became more likely than not. In September Japan took the first step in this plan and moved troops into northern Indo-China, by agreement with

Left: Germany, Japan and Italy sign the Tripartite Pact, September 1940.

the Vichy French. In return the Americans imposed an embargo on some iron and steel exports to Japan. A retaliatory process of escalation had begun.

Diplomatic preparations for new advances came with Japan's signing of the Tripartite Pact with Italy and Germany in September 1940. This was clearly aimed, from Japan's point of view, at limiting the USA's responses in the Pacific by the threat that such responses might involve the USA in a European war.

INTO INDO-CHINA

In July 1941 a Japanese government meeting decided to go into southern Indo-China as a first step to further moves south, even if this meant war. However, in the meantime, Japan would continue negotiations with the USA.

American code breakers read reports of the meeting; US leaders concluded that Japan had passed the point of no return, though in fact the Japanese were still uncertain. The Americans decided to step up their economic pressure, cutting

off almost all of Japan's oil supplies. This convinced the more militant Japanese that the USA had aggressive intentions, while at the same time they saw their stockpiles of strategic materials gradually diminishing.

Half-hearted negotiations continued into November but by then the new Japanese Prime Minister, General Tojo Hideki, and his government were convinced that their country had dithered for long enough. There seemed no serious possibility of agreement with the Americans without an unthinkable Japanese withdrawal from China. Japan still had a fighting chance, or so they believed, but they must take it immediately. On 29 November they made the decision to go to war.

Left: Soviet troops celebrate their decisive victory over Japan at Khalkhin Gol in 1939.

THE JAPANESE GOVERNMENT

To outsiders, Japan looked to be run in a similar way to countries like Britain, with an elected government and a ceremonial monarch. In fact in Japan the Army and Navy, and even factions within them, largely controlled national policy. The most militant officers were often those with least knowledge of the wider world, but their supposed patriotic motives were widely respected. Men of this kind had provoked the "Manchuria Incident" as far back as 1931, and ten years later their underestimation of US power would lead Japan into another disastrous war.

Above: Prince Konoye and General Tojo, Japan's last premiers before December 1941.

Left: Japanese troops extending their occupation of French Indo-China in August 1941.

Pearl Harbor and Japan's War Plans

Japan seemed to win a stunning victory at Pearl Harbor, but in the longer term the attack on sovereign United States territory, without a declaration of war, could hardly have been less in Japan's interests. The USA would fight on until victory.

On 7 December 1941 planes from six Japanese aircraft carriers made a surprise attack on the main base of the US Pacific Fleet at Pearl Harbor in Hawaii. Japan had not delivered a declaration of war when the attack began; the USA declared war on Japan the next day.

WHY PEARL HARBOR?

Japan's decision to attack Pearl Harbor came about in a round-about way. What Japan wanted was control of the natural resources of both the British and Dutch colonies in Malaysia and the East Indies.

KEY FACTS

PLACE: Oahu Island, Hawaii

DATE: 7 December 1941

OUTCOME: US Pacific Fleet crippled; USA and Japan go to war.

Below: Pearl Harbor at peace shortly before the Japanese attack. The Ford Island airstrip (centre) and "Battleship Row" to its left would be prime targets, but the oil storage tanks, further left, would be missed.

The Philippines, an American commonwealth, stood on the flank of such an advance and therefore would be attacked too, so war with the USA certainly had to be anticipated.

With Britain busy with the European war and the other colonial powers' homelands under German occupation, the main threat to Japan would come from the US Pacific Fleet – the US Navy was formidable though the US Army was not. Hence a strike on Pearl Harbor at the outset would gain time for Japan to grab the territory it sought. Japan would then fortify

Above: Japanese aircrew board their planes, ready to attack Pearl Harbor, 7 December 1941.

Above: The Ford Island airfield after the attack as ships in the harbour burn in the background.

a perimeter round its new empire which, Japan's leaders believed, would be so daunting that the feeble and decadent Americans would not dare to attack but instead make peace.

AMERICAN PRECAUTIONS

In the weeks before the attack the US government knew from code-breaking information that a Japanese military attack was very likely imminent. They thought that the most likely target would be the Philippines, and that the main danger to Hawaii was sabotage by Japanese agents. However, since the war it has been alleged that President Roosevelt and his government knew of the Japanese plans but did not take proper precautions, so they could mislead the American people into going to war. No real evidence for this claim exists.

From about 07:45 hours that Sunday morning, two waves of Japanese aircraft struck the naval anchorage and various air-fields on Oahu for two hours. By the end of the strikes, 2,403 Americans were dead, 6 of the 8 US battleships in port had been sunk, along with other vessels,

YAMAMOTO ISOROKU

Admiral Yamamoto (1884–1943) was Japan's principal naval commander of the war until his death in 1943, when his aircraft was intercepted by American fighters acting on code-breaking information. He had played a large part in the development of Japanese naval aviation before the war and was the architect of the Pearl Harbor attack. However, he had opposed going to war with the USA, saying that his fleet would win victories for the first few months, but after that Japan would certainly be crushed. His predictions were absolutely correct.

Above: Admiral Yamamoto working at his chart table.

and 188 American aircraft were destroyed. The Japanese lost 29 aircraft, 5 midget submarines and 1 larger submarine. On the US side a catalogue of errors had made Japan's task easier: radar warnings were ignored; anti-aircraft ammunition boxes were locked; and aircraft were easy targets on the ground because they had been parked together so they could be easily guarded against sabotage.

For the future there was now no doubt that, outraged by what President Roosevelt called "a day of infamy", the American people would fight and would continue their fight until their overwhelming resources had brought a total victory. And they also still had significant means to hand. The Pacific Fleet's air-craft carriers happened to be away from port that Sunday, a chance survival that would help point the way to the methods by which Japan would be defeated.

It was not just the Japanese who acted against their own best interests at Pearl Harbor. On 11 December 1941 Hitler declared war on the Americans. The USA now had to fight in the European war as well.

The USA at War

The war was kinder to the United States than to any other warring nation. The country ended the war with the lowest casualty rate of any major combatant and the American people generally prospered in the economic boom the war brought.

In late 1940 President Roosevelt spoke of his wish that the United States would become the "arsenal of democracy". Even before Pearl Harbor this wish was fast becoming a reality and its consequences were transforming the USA and its relationship with the rest of the world. No informed observer in 1939 was in any doubt about the country's potential strength, but when the war in Europe began 15 per cent of the workforce was unemployed, factories were idle and other economic indicators confirmed the gloomy picture.

By 1945 much had changed. In the course of the war the USA manufactured a stunning

Below: The Chrysler plant in Detroit, producing M3 tanks in 1942.

Above: Making aircraft engines was one of many new employment areas opened to American women.

total of 300,000 military aircraft, 86,000 tanks and vast amounts of every other conceivable kind of military equipment. The US armed forces were the most lavishly equipped in the world and, over and above their supplies, American production also met an estimated 25 per cent of British needs, 10 per cent of Soviet requirements and large proportions for every other Allied power.

Some 15 million men served in the US armed forces during the war along with 350,000 women, a total only surpassed by the Soviets. From 1942 this huge military establishment was controlled from the Pentagon, the world's largest building, which had been newly opened in Washington, DC.

At the heart of the Pentagon was another new body, the Joint Chiefs of Staff, the committee of the armed service chiefs, which co-ordinated American planning and had an effective liaison organization working with its British equivalent. Although there were many disputes, Anglo-American planning was much more effective than the chaotic German or Japanese equivalents, with their capricious leaders and vicious inter-service rivalries. The JCS organization was truly a major factor in the Allied victory.

In December 1941 Congress passed the War Powers Act giving the President more executive authority than he had ever had before. A whole range of government agencies was soon set up to manage various important aspects of the war economy – the War Production Board and Office of War Mobilization being among the most important. Manpower was perhaps the first issue. Conscription

Above: US rationing in 1941 was so lenient that this driver could fill a spare can as well as his tank.

never dug as deep in the USA as in many other countries – married men were seldom drafted, for example. Men not drafted did not have to take war jobs and women were not compelled to work or serve in any way.

Big business and ordinary people both prospered during the war. Corporate profits soared and so did farm prices. Wages rose 50 per cent in real terms. The number of women working outside the home also expanded by about a third to 22 per cent of the workforce. Previously, women in paid work had generally been young, unmarried or childless, but older women and mothers commonly took jobs during the war.

Although the idea of women doing "man's work" was much publicized, the reality was slightly different. Few women moving into the workforce took over jobs previously done by men; rather they took new jobs, often of types that had not commonly existed previously.

The archetypal character Rosie the Riveter working in a shipyard scarcely existed, if only because shipbuilding was rapidly moving to the more modern welding method of construction. Indeed at the heart of the war production boom were a mass of such productivity improvements: new technologies, better machine tools, greater use of assembly-line methods and more.

Although many women were working and prospering, they were still paid about a third less than men in comparable jobs. A similar situation applied to African-Americans and other racially disadvantaged groups. Their wages rose faster than those of whites during the war, but there was still a large gap and racism remained ubiquitous

JAPANESE-AMERICANS

In 1941 there were about 120,000 Japanese (over 60 per cent of them US citizens) living in the continental USA, and more than a third of the population of Hawaii was of Japanese descent. Though carefully watched, those in Hawaii were allowed to live normally. However, in early 1942, almost all Japanese living along the American West Coast were deported to a number of unpleasant detention camps inland and held there until late 1944. Fears of spying and sabotage were the official reason given, but the true motivation was a racist one. Canada also operated a similar policy for its Japanese population.

Above: Some 110,000 Japanese-Americans were sent to detention camps in 1942. German- and Italian-Americans were not similarly treated.

both in civilian life and in the military. Military units were racially segregated and few non-whites were permitted to serve in combat formations, and fewer still became officers.

Japan's First Advances

Japan's initial naval successes were soon matched by triumphs on land. Malaya and Britain's great naval base of Singapore were conquered with ease by mid-February 1942 and the final Allied bastion in the Philippines lasted little longer.

Simultaneously with the attack on Pearl Harbor, Japanese forces began operations against the Philippines and Malaya. The Japanese landings in Malaya began at 01:00 hours on 8 December 1941 (local time). This was actually shortly before the 7 December raid on Pearl Harbor because of the effects of the International Date Line. The first air attacks on Luzon in the Philippines came a few hours later.

As well as these major targets, the Japanese also began a rapid campaign to conquer Hong Kong, while other forces quickly took control of Guam, Wake and other small US-held islands, despite an energetic defence by Allied forces.

MALAYA UNDER ATTACK

The 65,000-strong Twenty-fifth Army, led by General Yamashita Tomoyuki, began its campaign

Above: Although outdated by European standards, Japanese tanks like this Type 95, in action on Luzon, led their advance in 1942.

with landings on the South China Sea coast of northern Malaya and southern Siam (now Thailand). They were opposed by almost 90,000 British, Indian and Australian troops under the overall command of Air Marshal Robert Brooke-Popham, with General Arthur Percival as land commander. The Japanese quickly gained command of the

air and, after sinking HMS *Prince of Wales* and *Repulse*, had complete control at sea.

Many of the Japanese troops were battle-hardened veterans of the China war but, contrary to popular belief, they had had no special jungle training. They had a few tanks to break up any defensive positions they met and bicycles for mobility. By contrast the Allied troops were mostly badly trained and poorly led at almost every level. The result was that the Allied forces were hustled into retreat, time after time.

FALL OF SINGAPORE

By the end of January 1942 the Allied forces had withdrawn to Singapore island, over 950km (590 miles) from the initial Japanese landings. Singapore was supposedly an impregnable fortress, but its defences had been built with a naval attack in

SINKING OF FORCE Z

As relations with Japan deteriorated in late 1941, the British government decided to send naval reinforcements ("Force Z") to Singapore to deter Japanese action. Two battleships, the *Prince of Wales* and *Repulse*, were sent but a planned aircraft carrier did not go. The admiral in charge was one of the least air-minded in the Royal Navy; he made a blundering attempt, without air cover, to intercept Japanese landing forces off Malaya. Instead, on 10 December, the British ships were tracked down and sunk with little difficulty by Japanese land-based aircraft.

Above: *Prince of Wales*, *Repulse* and an escorting destroyer (nearest) seen from a Japanese aircraft.

mind and were not well suited to opposing an advance across the Johor Straits to the north.

On the night of 8–9 February the Japanese surged over and soon pushed the defenders back to the edges of Singapore city itself. General Percival decided to capitulate, though his troops (recently reinforced) greatly outnumbered their attackers.

In the whole Malayan campaign the Japanese lost fewer than 10,000 casualties. The Allies had a similar number of killed and wounded, but in addition some 130,000 went into a brutal Japanese captivity that many would not survive.

THE PHILIPPINES

Japan's conquest of the Philippines was almost as rapid. General Douglas MacArthur led the defending forces of 110,000 Filipino troops and 30,000 Americans, though inevitably many were dispersed around the Philippine archipelago. Equipment and training were poor but they did have over 200 supporting American aircraft. However, MacArthur's incompetence allowed many of these to be surprised on the ground hours after news of Pearl Harbor arrived. From then on Japan had control in the air. With no prospect of relieving US Navy forces arriving, as pre-Pearl Harbor plans had anticipated, Japan was also dominant at sea.

Troops from General Homma Masaharu's Fourteenth Army landed on the main island of Luzon on 10 December with

Right: Surrender of Singapore, 15 February 1942. General Yamashita insists that General Percival signs without further delay.

larger forces following from the 22nd. MacArthur ordered the outmatched Allied troops to withdraw to the Bataan Peninsula area, which they did by early January 1942.

They held out there until 9 April, in part because some of the attacking Japanese troops had been withdrawn to take part in other phases of Japan's offensive. The fortress island of Corregidor offshore did not

Above: American and Filipino soldiers under fire in the defences of the Bataan Peninsula.

surrender until 6 May. Again many Allied troops were sent into a cruel captivity.

Meanwhile, MacArthur had been ordered to leave in mid-March to take command of Allied forces in Australia. On his departure MacArthur had promised: "I shall return."

Japan's Continuing Successes

Even before Malaya and the Philippines had fallen, Japanese forces were surging into Burma and landing throughout the Dutch East Indies. Their campaigns there would be just as rapid and successful as those that had gone before.

Japanese troops moved into Burma on 14 December 1941. An attack began in earnest on 20 January 1942 when General Iida Shojiro's Fifteenth Army launched two divisions toward Moulmein from across the border with Thailand. Allied forces fought effectively at first, retreating gradually. On 23 February a vital bridge over the River Sittang was blown up with many Indian troops on the wrong side. After that the retreat turned into a rout.

The Japanese were reinforced with troops from Malaya, now that campaign was over, and Rangoon fell on 8 March. Further Japanese troops then moved in from Thailand, and pushed the remaining British forces northward toward India. Chinese troops, commanded by an American, General Joseph Stilwell, joined in the battle but

Above: Apprehensive Burmese wait by the roadside as Japanese invaders pass by.

Below: Japanese Type 89 tanks on the advance in 1942. Lightly armoured and with a low-powered 57mm (2.24in) gun, the Type 89 was mainly used in China later in the war.

were also defeated. The last remnants of the Allied force reached India in early May.

VITAL OILFIELDS

The Dutch East Indies was the greatest prize in Japan's planned advance because of its substantial oilfields, mainly on Sumatra, and the significant production of metal ores and other important commodities. Japan's air and naval superiority was the key to their advance.

There were three main lines of attack, with various units from General Imamura Hitoshi's Sixteenth Army providing the principal ground forces. Sixteenth Army had first moved from Japanese possessions in the Caroline Islands to the southern Philippine island of Mindanao. In early January it struck toward Borneo and the Celebes, using both paratroops and forces landed by sea, before

Left: Japanese infantry capturing the Yenangyaung oilfields in Burma in April 1942. Gaining access to foreign oil was a key Japanese aim.

leap-frogging south to Timor and eastern Java. At the same time other forces landed along Borneo's northern coast and by late February/early March were in Sumatra and western Java. Local Dutch and other Allied forces surrendered on 8 March.

NEW NAVAL VICTORIES

There were a number of naval engagements during the campaign, fought on the Allied side by Dutch, British, Australian and US Navy ships, led by the Dutch Admiral Karel Doorman. The Allied force was defeated on 27 February 1942 in the Battle of the Java Sea, and wiped out in follow-up engagements over the next two days.

Australian-ruled territory had also fallen. In January the Japanese captured Rabaul on New Britain (part of Australia's New Guinea mandated territory) and would build up a major base there. On 19 February they further demonstrated their naval superiority in the theatre when four of the aircraft carriers from the Pearl Harbor attack force led a devastating raid on Darwin in Northern Australia. On 8 March Japanese troops landed at Lae and Salamaua in New Guinea proper, as the first stage in a planned advance to Port Moresby on Papua's south coast.

Having supported various of the Japanese landings, the carrier force then moved further west in March to attack Ceylon and British Indian Ocean trade. The main British and Japanese naval forces did not come into action against each other, but two British cruisers and a small aircraft carrier were sunk. The ports of Colombo and Trincomalee were heavily raided, while a subsidiary Japanese force sank numerous merchant ships in the Bay of Bengal.

Japan had achieved a bewildering succession of victories across a vast area, but ambitious generals and admirals planned still more advances. First they planned to attack New Guinea and then (stung by the American pinprick Doolittle Raid on the Japanese Home Islands) they would advance across the central Pacific to Midway.

THE DOOLITTLE RAID

In early 1942 US aircraft carriers began striking back at Japan with minor raids on various Pacific islands. In April a more ambitious plan, an attack on Tokyo, was carried out. On 18 April the carrier *Hornet* launched 16 Army Air Force B-25 bombers, commanded by Colonel James Doolittle, from some 1,000km (625 miles) offshore. Minor damage was caused in the Japanese capital and three other cities. The raid was a major boost to domestic morale in the USA and helped persuade Japan's leaders to carry out what proved to be their disastrous attack on Midway.

Below: A B-25 sets out for Tokyo. Taking off in a B-25 from a carrier was a remarkable feat, but no naval aircraft had the range needed for this mission.

Coral Sea and Midway

These two battles were the first naval engagements in history in which the opposing ships never came into visual contact. They confirmed that aircraft carriers were now the dominant weapons in naval warfare.

As May 1942 began, Japanese commanders planned to extend their conquests by landing at Port Moresby in southern Papua, from where their aircraft might reach targets in Australia. Warned by code-breaking information, Allied naval forces were sent to stop them.

Leading the Allied force were the US carriers *Lexington* and *Yorktown*, supported by American and Australian cruisers and destroyers. Opposing them were three main Japanese forces: the Port Moresby invasion force of troop transports and escorts; a covering force

KEY FACTS–MIDWAY

PLACE: Central Pacific, near Midway Island

DATE: 4 June 1942

OUTCOME: 4 Japanese aircraft carriers sunk; Japanese naval superiority lost.

THE BATTLE OF MIDWAY

As in other battles in the Pacific, the Japanese plan for Midway was over-complicated and failed to concentrate on the main objective.

including the small carrier *Shoho* and four cruisers; and a carrier strike force based around the *Zuikaku* and *Shokaku*. Also a small detachment was to land on Tulagi in the Solomon Islands to set up a base there.

CORAL SEA BATTLE

After preliminary skirmishes, the main action began on 7 May. US aircraft sank the *Shoho*; in return the Japanese carriers sank an American tanker and a destroyer. A full-scale carrier battle followed on the 8th. The Japanese came off better, sinking the *Lexington* and damaging

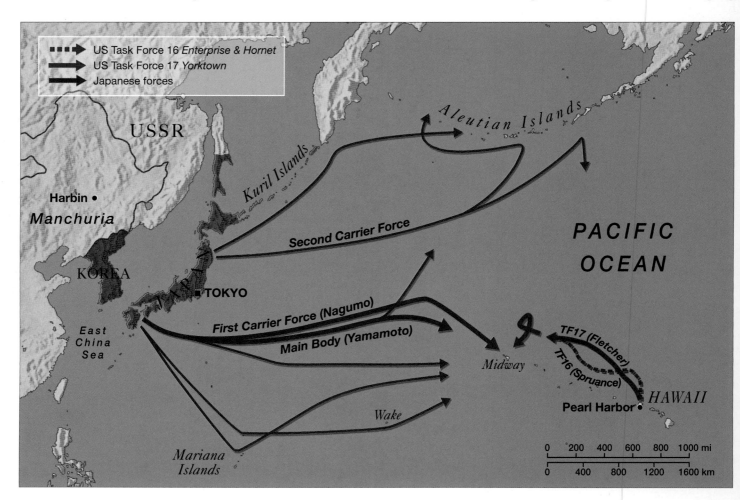

the *Yorktown* badly. However, the *Shokaku* was also heavily hit and many of the *Zuikaku*'s aircraft were destroyed. Neither ship would be able to join the Midway operation, which was scheduled next, and the Port Moresby invasion was called off.

THE MIDWAY PLAN

Admiral Yamamoto, principal Japanese Navy commander, had realized for some time that his victory at Pearl Harbor was incomplete unless he could destroy the US Navy's carrier force. He planned to capture Midway, far across the Central Pacific toward Pearl Harbor, confident that this move would force the Americans into battle.

The Japanese plan was characteristically complicated, with a selection of transport and covering forces closing in on Midway from various directions. Two smaller carriers and other major warships were to carry out a diversion against the Aleutian Islands, while the main forces included four carriers and a battleship and cruiser group.

Unfortunately for the Japanese, their intentions had once again been discovered by the US code-breaking services. The Americans were, therefore, able to ignore the Aleutians force (whose valuable carriers were thus wasted) and concentrate their strongest units near Midway before the Japanese knew they were in the area. The Americans deployed the carriers *Hornet* and *Enterprise* and supporting vessels, which were joined at the last minute by the rapidly repaired *Yorktown* (which the Japanese were convinced would be out of action for much longer).

Above: The Japanese carrier *Shokaku* under attack and on fire during the Coral Sea battle.

The main action began early on 4 June with Japanese air attacks on Midway Island. Thinking these attacks had not been successful enough and unaware for the moment of the American carriers' presence, Admiral Nagumo Chuichi, commanding the Japanese carriers, then ordered preparations for another attack on Midway.

While this was happening, attack aircraft from Midway Island and then from the American carriers arrived. Most were easily dealt with by the Japanese fighter screen, but a final dive-bomber group from the *Enterprise* inflicted crippling damage on *Akagi*, *Kaga* and

Above: A Japanese torpedo strikes home on the *Yorktown* at Midway, despite defensive anti-aircraft fire.

Soryu (all three would sink later). The fourth Japanese carrier, *Hiryu*, sent a new strike that badly damaged *Yorktown*, but later *Hiryu* was itself fatally hit. Yamamoto abandoned the Midway operation.

Even though *Yorktown* was sunk on 7 June by a Japanese submarine, Midway had been a stunning American success. The backbone of the Japanese fleet was destroyed; not only the lost ships but also the many well-trained aircrew would not be readily replaced.

Below: A Devastator torpedo-bomber squadron ready for take-off on the *Enterprise* at Midway.

The Turn of the Tide

*Desperate struggles in the Solomon Islands and on New Guinea from mid-1942
saw the Japanese advance turned back for the first time. The Allies gained the
upper hand in vicious jungle fighting and a series of dramatic naval battles.*

Having overrun the East Indies so easily, Japan then planned to capture bases in southern Papua, as a prelude to a possible attack on Australia and others in the Solomon Islands, to threaten communications between Australia and the USA. As well as Australian and American ground and air forces, the resulting battles would draw in the main strength of both the Japanese and US Navies.

NEW GUINEA

After Japan's naval attack was thwarted in the Battle of the Coral Sea, General Horii Tomitaro's South Seas Detachment began an advance in July 1942 from the north coast of Papua over the precipitous Owen Stanley Range on the Kokoda Trail toward Port Moresby. Despite the terrible conditions (for both sides) the Japanese soon pushed back the weak Australian forces, now part of General MacArthur's Allied South-West Pacific Command. Allied air power and some reinforcements halted Horii on the approaches to Port Moresby in September and the Japanese retreated (so short of supplies some resorted to cannibalism).

In the meantime Allied air and naval forces had begun advances round the eastern tip of Papua, beginning at Milne Bay in August. By November Australian troops attacking along the Kokoda Trail and American troops moving along

Above: A wounded Australian near Buna is helped by a Papuan, one of many who assisted the Allied forces.

COAST WATCHERS

The Australian Navy used Coast Watchers, people who provided vital information to Allied forces during the Solomons campaign and other battles. The service had been set up before the war to cover a range of locations across the little-inhabited South-west Pacific. From their lonely and isolated posts, Coast Watchers reported movements by air and sea and also supplied weather reports, which was often just as important. Though they had to defend themselves against Japanese patrols, their role was not to fight. Admiral Halsey said that Guadalcanal would not have been won without their help.

---

the north coast had closed in on the well-fortified Japanese beachheads at Buna and Gona. The remaining Japanese forces there were wiped out by the end of January 1943.

Guadalcanal Island, the focus of the other flank of the campaign, saw conditions that were just as horrible. Japan had set up a seaplane base at nearby Tulagi in May and a small force was working on an airfield on Guadalcanal itself. The 1st US Marine Division landed on Guadalcanal on 7 August 1942, captured the airfield and put it into Allied service as Henderson Field. At first the Marines were not well supported from the sea; Japanese reinforcements began attacking the Marines' beach-head. During the six-month struggle that followed the Japanese troops fought fiercely, but their attacks were not well co-ordinated and were beaten off after a series of tough battles. Japan evacuated the island in early February 1943.

NAVAL BATTLES

Both sides' efforts to supply and reinforce their troops led to six major naval battles and a range of smaller engagements. At first the Japanese had the upper hand. In the early hours of 9 August, in the Battle of Savo Island, night-fighting skills and superior torpedo equipment helped a group of Japanese cruisers and destroyers sink four opponents with little loss.

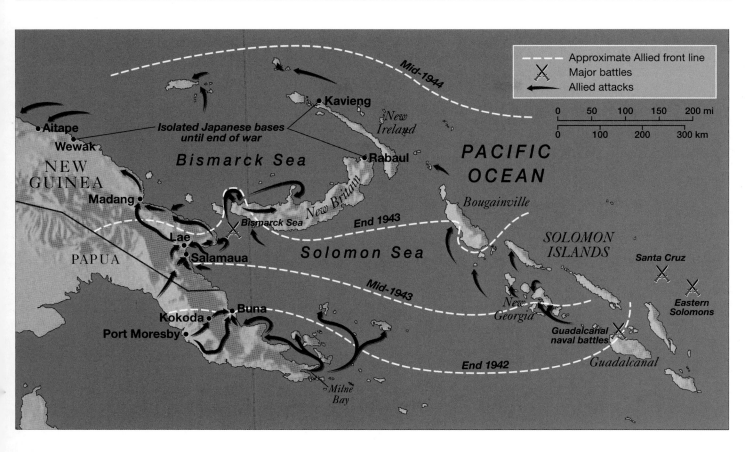

THE SOUTH-WEST PACIFIC

From summer 1942, Allied forces conducted a two-pronged advance along the north coast of New Guinea and up the Solomon Island chain.

On 23–4 August the Battle of the Eastern Solomons between the main carrier forces was a narrow Japanese victory; and in subsequent weeks two US carriers were sunk by submarines. However, by then aircraft from Henderson Field dominated the waters around Guadalcanal by day; but at night Japanese warships under Admiral Tanaka Raizo, known to the Marines as the "Tokyo Express", had the ascendancy.

A second carrier battle on 26 October, the Battle of Santa Cruz, was inconclusive, but the tide turned with the Battle of Guadalcanal taking place on the

Right: A Japanese bomb explodes aboard the *Enterprise* during the Battle of the Eastern Solomons.

nights of 12–13 and 14–15 November. By then the American forces were learning to use their superior radar equipment to win night battles. The fighting between the warships was by no means one-sided but several Japanese troop transports were sunk. The Japanese had the better of another night encounter (the Battle of Tassafaronga) in late November. However, by then the attrition of their naval forces had become so severe that in early January the Tokyo Express finally went into reverse – to evacuate rather than supply the island. The Allied counter-offensive in the Pacific was now well under way.

Japan's Brutal Empire

Japan's military conquests were supported by an authoritarian military government at home and ruthless exploitation of the people and resources of the conquered territories, though this was disguised by anti-imperialist propaganda.

In 1938 Japan's Prime Minister, Prince Konoye Fumimaro, spoke of Japan's aim to create a "New Order" in Asia. In 1940, after a period out of office, Konoye returned as premier and announced Japan's plan to establish a Greater East Asia Co-Prosperity Sphere. These ideas, and their slogan "Asia for the Asiatics" formed part of the backdrop to the creation of Japan's wartime empire. European and American racism and imperialism were to be rejected in favour of a vague commonwealth from which all Asians were to benefit – ideas that were designed to appeal both at home in Japan and throughout Asia.

MILITARISM AT HOME

From the later 1920s Japan itself became an ever more militaristic and rigorously regimented

Above: A Japanese soldier proudly displays the severed head of a Chinese man, Shanghai, 1937.

Below: From 1941 Japanese high-school students had compulsory military training in the curriculum.

society. The armed services took effective control of the government. As well as expanding Japan's war in China, factions within the army had no hesitation in assassinating opponents or planning military coups. The economy was increasingly industrialized and militarized, with businesses and trades unions also brought under government control.

The education system emphasized military and nationalistic values: for example, maps in school textbooks showed much of South-east Asia as rightfully forming part of Japan's Empire. And in the background were the Tokko, or Special Higher Police (usually referred to in English as the "Thought Police"), who used torture and other repressive methods to ensure citizens behaved as the government wished.

CRUELTY ABROAD

The reality of Japan's rule overseas belied the intent expressed in Konoye's slogans. Most obvious to the Western Allies was its treatment of prisoners of war. Japanese troops were taught that it was disgraceful to surrender and regarded with contempt any enemy who did so. Many American prisoners, captured in the Philippines in 1942, died of ill-treatment on the so-called Bataan Death March and around 12,000 British and Australians were starved, beaten and worked to death on the

Above: Ho Chi Minh, leader of the anti-Japanese resistance movement in Indo-China, was helped by US special forces later in the war.

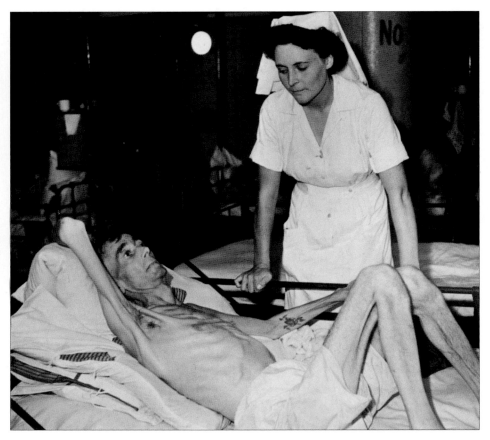

Above: An emaciated British prisoner receives medical treatment after his liberation from Japanese-occupied Hong Kong in 1945.

Siam–Burma railway line, to give only two of numerous notorious examples.

However, if only because relatively few Westerners came into Japanese hands, these brutalities bear little comparison with those inflicted on other Asians – for example, as many as 90,000 Malaysian, Thai and other Asian labourers died on the Burma Railway. Japan's attitude to other Asians was more brutal, racist and exploitative than any of the much-despised colonial powers.

The outside world first became aware of this with the infamous "Rape of Nanking", in December 1937, which was widely reported elsewhere. When Japanese troops captured the town (now usually called Nanjing), they went on an extended rampage of murder, rape, looting and arson, which killed a quarter of a million people (according to some estimates). Throughout the war in China, Japanese tactics made no distinction between civilians and military opponents; the watchwords were the "three alls" – kill all, burn all, loot all.

Other Japanese methods were more insidious. In the puppet state of Manchukuo, for example, the Japanese authorities encouraged and greatly expanded the production of opium. They also pushed users of opium there and in the rest of China to switch to the more dangerous morphine and heroin compounds, as part of a deliberate strategy to keep the indigenous population docile. The revenues from the scheme were used for the benefit of Japan's Kwantung Army.

For all that Japanese rule was far harsher than the colonial regimes that had preceded it, it also discredited such pre-war governments. In the aftermath Asia would soon come to be ruled by Asiatics to an extent unimaginable before.

COMFORT WOMEN

One of the nastiest aspects of Japanese rule was the imposition of forced prostitution on many thousands of mainly non-Japanese women. In part to prevent atrocities like the mass rapes that had occurred at Nanjing, the Japanese Army set up official military brothels in China and elsewhere. Up to 200,000 women worked in these establishments and many of them were teenagers. They were supposed to receive payments, but many were forced into unpaid prostitution. Most of the women were Korean.

The Holocaust Emaciated survivors shortly after the liberation of Buchenwald camp in 1945.

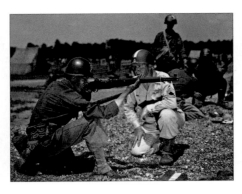

Infantry Weapons An American infantryman training with his M1 Garand semi-automatic rifle.

US Strategic Bombing, 1942–3 A B-24 Liberator falls in flames after being hit by flak.

Incorporated in Hitler's Reich
German-occupied 23 June 1
German allies 1942–44
Neutrals
Front line 5 Dec 1941
Front line May 1942
Front line 18 Nov 1942
Front line 4 July 1943
Front line 23 June 1944

| 0 | 100 | 200 | 300 | 400 | 500 mi |
| 0 | 200 | 400 | 600 | | 800 km |

ICELAND

ATLANTIC OCEAN

NORWAY

SWEDEN

FINLAND

USSR

North Sea

IRELAND

UNITED KINGDOM

DENMARK

Baltic Sea

ESTONIA

LATVIA

LITHUANIA

EAST PRUSSIA

NETHER-LANDS

BELGIUM

GERMANY

POLAND

CZECHOSLOVAKIA

FRANCE

SWITZER-LAND

AUSTRIA

HUNGARY

ROMANIA

YUGOSLAVIA

ALBANIA

BULGARIA

Black Sea

PORTUGAL

SPAIN

Corsica

Sardinia

ITALY

8 Oct 1943

15 Jan 1943

Sicily

17 Aug 1943

GREECE

TURKEY

SYRIA (French)

CYPRUS (British)

IRAQ (Britis)

Mediterranean Sea

TUNISIA (French)

PALESTINE (British)

TRANS-JORDAN (British)

ALGERIA (French)

15 Jan 1943

1 Jan 1942

18 Nov 1941

31 Aug 1942

North Africa front lines

LIBYA (Italian)

EGYPT (British)

THE GREAT STRUGGLE IN EUROPE

Just as his forces were being pushed back from Moscow in December 1941, Hitler assured his eventual defeat by declaring war on the USA. By the middle of 1944 Axis troops had been thrown out of the USSR and expelled from Africa; Italy had made peace; Anglo-American bombers were pounding Germany from the air; and Allied land forces were poised to return across the Channel in the Normandy invasion. Yet, between these landmarks, there lay many hard-fought campaigns and much dreadful suffering.

This was the period when the Nazi murder campaign against Europe's Jews was at its height. The Eastern Front saw the horrific sieges of Leningrad and Stalingrad and the war's greatest tank battle at Kursk. The Western Allies gradually grew in confidence and strength, initially in their victories in North Africa, then in their burgeoning power at sea and in the air that made first Hitler's Kriegsmarine, and then the Luftwaffe, shadows of the forces they had once been.

In his post-war memoirs Churchill wrote that the Allied victory was inevitable from the moment the USA joined the war. In hindsight this may indeed have been true, but it took the vicious battles of 1942–4 to turn this judgement into a reality.

Assault Guns An American soldier examines a German Jagdpanther knocked out in 1945.

Clearing the Ukraine Red Army troops being welcomed warmly on their recapture of Kiev.

Naval Weapons and Electronics Guns on the foredeck of the battleship USS *Iowa*.

To Stalingrad and the Caucasus

Despite their losses in the first terrible winter of war on the Eastern Front, the Germans were ready to attack again in 1942. Once more they used their superior tactical skills to win early successes, but a final decisive victory remained elusive.

After pushing the Germans back from Moscow with their December 1941 counter-offensive, the Soviets tried to develop a general advance all along the Eastern Front. Although these attacks created large bulges into German-held territory, the major German defensive positions held with relatively little difficulty. By the time the spring thaw brought operations to a halt, it was clear that the Germans would attack again in strength that summer.

Although the German forces had been substantially reinforced by troops from Hungary, Romania, Italy and even Spain, they no longer had the power to attack over the whole Eastern Front. Instead Hitler decided to concentrate in the south. He chose two objectives: a drive into the Caucasus as far as the

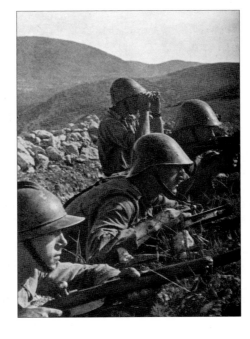

Above: Romanian troops in action in the Crimea alongside their German allies in June–July 1942.

Below: German infantry advancing during their successful counter-offensive near Kharkov in late May.

Caspian coast to gain control of the oilfields there, and an advance to Stalingrad (Volgograd) to establish a protective front along the Don River north to Voronezh.

PRELIMINARY ATTACKS

Late spring and early summer saw new German successes. Attacks in the Crimea led by General Erich von Manstein wiped out Soviet forces on the Kerch Peninsula in May and took Sevastopol by early July. To the north a Soviet attack near Kharkov in mid-May was crushed. Together these operations saw a further 450,000 prisoners fall into German hands.

The main German attacks began on 28 June. Voronezh was captured within days as the Soviet front at first fell apart before the German attacks. By late July other German attacks captured Rostov and opened the way south into the Caucasus.

However, Hitler was already changing his mind on priorities and readjusting his forces. In mid-July General Friedrich Paulus's Sixth Army had been told to rush east toward Stalingrad and much of the tank forces of Fourth Panzer Army, which had been meant to lead the drive into the Caucasus, were switched to join the right flank of Sixth Army's advance. To complete the range of contradictory objectives, Hitler also ordered Manstein's victorious troops from the Crimea to

THE GERMAN ADVANCE TO STALINGRAD

German advances in the summer of 1942 greatly lengthened their front line but made no decisive gains.

Above: German troops at Maykop in late summer 1942. Retreating Soviets have set the oil wells alight.

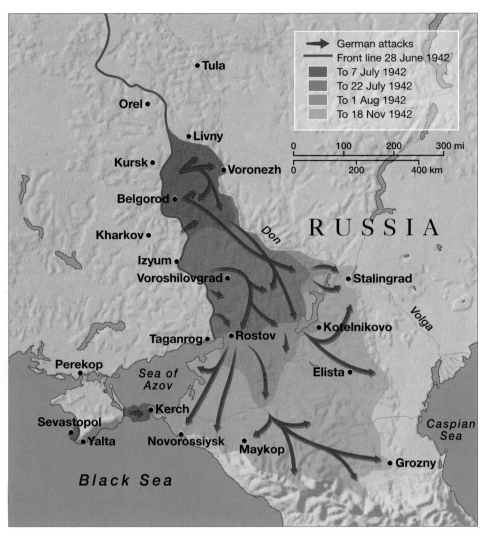

move north to Leningrad to finish the destruction of the Soviet resistance there.

SOVIET RESPONSES

For his part Stalin had misjudged the direction of the German attacks, fearing an advance toward Moscow from the south and, accordingly, had not deployed his reserves well.

However, the general Soviet organization had greatly improved. New production was being used to create air and tank armies that might provide a proper answer to German power in these respects, while more authority was being given to commanders to control their operations without political interference from their unit commissars. Finally, a group of ruthless and efficient generals was becoming established in

senior positions, who would make good use of the ever-stronger Soviet forces.

For the moment the German advance continued. By early August, Sixth Army was destroying the Soviet forces in the Don bend, west of Stalingrad. By the end of the month it had reached the Volga, linked up with Fourth Panzer Army and closed to within a handful of kilometres of the city. Meanwhile, with supplies and air support having been switched to the Stalingrad sector, the advance in the Caucasus had ground to a halt, short of most of its objectives and never to be resumed. For Hitler and for Stalin, capturing or holding Stalingrad was now the only objective that mattered.

Below: A German tank unit halted in the vast and featureless steppe, south of Stalingrad, is overflown by a liaison aircraft.

The Holocaust

In a war of many atrocities one series of actions stands out as particularly horrific – Nazi Germany's attempt, at Hitler's command, to murder all the Jews of Europe solely because of their race and religion.

There are aspects of the vast history of WWII in which a simple factual account seems inadequate. The list of Jews murdered by the Nazis – at least 2.5 million Poles, 750,000 from the USSR, almost as many each from Hungary and Romania, and tens of thousands more from almost every occupied country in Europe – cannot begin to explain the suffering and vile cruelties involved. At the same time, however, failing to state what happened and how it came to happen can only assist those who would downscale or even deny the nature of these crimes.

Above: Jewish families are taken from the Warsaw ghetto, probably to the Treblinka death camp.

EARLY PERSECUTIONS

Although Jews in pre-war Germany, and in occupied western Europe in 1940–1, were viciously persecuted, there were few killings. Eastern Europe presented, from the Nazi point of view, a different problem. They aimed to make their domains "Jew-free" and here there were many more Jews to deal with. During 1940 most Polish Jews were forced to live in "ghettos" in major towns. These were deliberately made overcrowded and insanitary and a typical food ration was less than 200 calories per day. By the middle of 1941 the half-million Jews in the Warsaw ghetto were dying at the rate of 2,000 daily.

Even this did not satisfy the Nazis. The armies invading the USSR were closely followed by *Einsatzgruppen* – SS murder

Left: An *Einsatzgruppe* killer at work, murdering Jews at Vinnitsa in the Ukraine in 1941–2.

squads whose mission was to kill Jews and communists. By the end of 1941 at least 600,000 Jews had been rounded up, shot and tumbled into mass graves. This was done quite openly, often watched and photographed by German Army soldiers and other personnel.

THE FINAL SOLUTION

By this stage leading Nazis were looking for a "final solution to the Jewish problem", by which they meant finding an easy way to murder all of the Jews in Europe. The process began in the autumn of 1941 and was put into high gear by a meeting of top Nazis – known as the Wannsee Conference – in January 1942.

The killing mostly took place in specially established death camps in occupied Poland.

From late 1941 Jews from the Polish ghettos were transported to the camps and gassed, followed later by transports from the rest of German-controlled Europe. Most of the camps killed Jews as soon as they arrived but the largest, Auschwitz-Birkenau, sent only a portion to the gas chambers immediately and worked most of the remainder to death in a range of factories. Survivors from the camps were marched west in 1944, as the Red Army approached, to endure yet more slave labour. A few emaciated victims were liberated in 1945.

Most of the Jews of Germany, Poland and the western USSR died, but elsewhere the picture was less uniform. The Bulgarian government refused to allow any Jews to be sent to the camps, Mussolini's regime largely left them alone, and almost all of Denmark's Jews were smuggled to neutral Sweden, for example.

In all countries many people risked their lives to help Jews, both on a small and larger scale. By contrast some in France's Vichy government willingly assisted in the deportation process, and most countries had collaborators who helped the Nazis in their dirty work. Many Germans later denied knowing anything of what had been done in their name (indeed the Nazis tried to keep secret what was happening in the camps), but the official Nazi explanation that the Jews were taken east for "resettlement" cannot really have fooled many people.

Right: Adolf Eichmann, the callous bureaucrat who managed much of the "Final Solution".

Britain and the USA had a fair idea of what was happening from the middle of 1942 but, other than a few protests, did nothing that might have slowed or halted the murders. Although since blamed on anti-semitism, this failure probably arose because it was so difficult to accept the appalling truth that 6 million Jews were being killed.

Above: Some of the survivors liberated from Buchenwald in 1945, including the Nobel Laureate Elie Wiesel, middle bunk, seventh from the left.

EUTHANASIA

Many of the techniques of mass murder used against the Jews had been developed for use in the Nazi euthanasia programmes. During the 1930s over 300,000 carriers of hereditary mental illnesses or disabilities were sterilized. From 1939 onwards, over 100,000 "inferior Germans" were callously murdered, many by the medical staff of the hospitals "caring" for them. Victims included senile patients, the insane and infants with physical handicaps or genetic conditions such as Down's syndrome.

Stalingrad

The Battle of Stalingrad is rightly regarded as the turning point of WWII. Before then any defeats suffered by Germany were little more than minor setbacks; after the Stalingrad calamity, rant at his generals as he might, Hitler had lost the war.

As the German advance ground toward Stalingrad through the summer of 1942, the war came to the local people in earnest. Stalin at first forbade any evacuation of the civilian population to prevent any suggestion that the city was likely to fall. Work continued in factories that produced the weapons that could be used immediately. T-34s from the former tractor factory would be driven straight into battle, unpainted and often lacking gunsights. Men not already in the army were formed into militia units and sent, untrained, straight into action with predictable horrendous

Below: German infantry armed with submachine-guns prepare to attack amid the ruins of Stalingrad.

KEY FACTS

PLACE: Stalingrad

DATE: 12 September 1942–
2 February 1943

OUTCOME: German Sixth Army failed to capture the city and was itself annihilated.

---

casualties. Women and children toiled to dig trenches and build defences; other women crewed anti-aircraft guns.

ATTACKING THE CITY

On 12 September the first German troops moved into the city itself. The Germans chose to attack straight into the urban area and soon became embroiled in a vicious house-to-house battle. Soviet tactics were to establish front-line positions as close as possible to the German lines – the safest place from German air and artillery attack.

At the end of August Stalin had sent his top general, Georgi Zhukov, to supervise the whole southern front and now a new commander, Vasili Chuikov, took over 62nd Army in the city itself. While Zhukov prepared for an eventual counter-offensive, Chuikov drove his troops relentlessly into combat. A steady stream of reinforcements was ferried under fire across the Volga into the ruins, just enough arriving (despite repeated crises) to keep at least part of the city in Soviet hands.

Above: General Vasili Chuikov, the tough commander of 62nd Army in the defence of Stalingrad.

Underlying the desperate defence of Stalingrad was the brutal and merciless disciplinary system of the Red Army. In August 1941 Stalin had issued an order that anyone trying to surrender should be shot on the spot. On 28 July 1942 his Order 227 (known as "Not One Step Backwards") reinforced this message. Armies were to form a second line of troops behind an attack to shoot anyone who wavered. Officers who "allowed" their men to desert or troops cut off by the Germans but who later returned to Soviet lines were sent to punishment battalions, a virtual death sentence. At least 400,000 died in such units in the course of the war.

Soviet losses were huge, but German casualties mounted, too. At the end of September, and again in mid-October, the Germans came close to victory, but the defenders just clung on in a small part of the city's northern factory district.

GERMAN VULNERABILITY

The advance to Stalingrad had brought other consequences for the Axis forces. In the course of the summer Hitler had sacked several of his top generals after quarrels about the strategic plan. Now he himself took many command decisions, both big and small. The advance to Stalingrad had greatly lengthened the German front and, as a consequence, two Romanian armies and an Italian army had been brought into line on the flanks of Sixth Army and Fourth Panzer Army. The Romanian troops were poorly motivated and trained and very badly equipped. They would be the first targets for the planned Soviet counter-offensive.

The Soviets attacked north of Stalingrad on 19 November and to the south the next day. The Romanian fronts were shattered. Within a week the two advancing Red Army forces had joined up and cut Stalingrad off. General Paulus asked for permission to break out – and at that stage could almost certainly have done so – but Hitler refused, promising to supply the trapped troops by air. General Erich von Manstein was brought in to lead a relief attempt that nearly reached the surrounded pocket, but he had to retreat just before Christmas.

In the meantime the air supply effort to Stalingrad's frozen airfields had cost the Luftwaffe hundreds of transport aircraft and delivered only a fraction of

Above: Last survivors of the German Stalingrad garrison march off into Soviet captivity.

the necessary supplies. Short of fuel and ammunition and slowly starving, Sixth Army now faced superior forces on all sides. The end was inevitable. The last German troops in the city surrendered on 2 February 1943.

Above: German Stukas in action over Stalingrad in the early stages of the siege, autumn 1942.

Soviet Winter Victories, 1942–3

Inspired by their success around Stalingrad, Soviet attacks continued through the winter of 1942–3. Now stronger and better-equipped than ever before, they regained all the territory that had been lost during 1942.

The encirclement of Stalingrad and the eventual destruction of the German Sixth Army was only part of a more general Soviet offensive all along the southern Eastern Front in the winter of 1942–3.

General Manstein's attempt to relieve Stalingrad began on 12 December 1942 and made good progress at first, despite the bitter winter weather. Within days, however, new Soviet attacks on his flanks were posing an additional threat. The Italian Eighth Army to the north

Left: General Konstantin Rokossovsky commanded the Don Front around Stalingrad in 1942–3.

was smashed, even as the forces moving toward Stalingrad were being slowed by fierce resistance. By the end of the year Manstein's units were in retreat. To the south the Soviet Stalingrad Front (or Army Group) was striking toward Rostov to cut the German Army Group A off in the Caucasus; the Don Front was tightening the ring around Stalingrad; and the South-West Front was freeing the whole area to the west of the great Don River bend.

NEW SOVIET ATTACKS

In January the Soviet attacks were extended to the north. Once again troops from one of Germany's satellites were the initial target. Voronezh Front smashed into Hungarian Second Army, as weak and ill-equipped as its Italian and Romanian counterparts. Within days the Hungarian force had been effectively destroyed and German Second Army to its north had also been pushed back.

Off to the south Hitler had delayed giving Army Group A permission to retreat from the Caucasus. The motorized units of First Panzer Army managed

WINTER BATTLES, 1942–3
Despite their brief recovery at Kharkov, the winter battles were disastrous for the German forces.

Map

Legend:
- Soviet attacks
- German attacks Feb–Mar 1943
- Front line 18 Nov 1942
- Front line 13 Dec 1942
- Front line 18 Jan 1943
- Soviet-held end Mar 1943
- Farthest Soviet advances mid-Feb 1943

Scale: 0 — 100 — 200 — 300 mi
0 — 200 — 400 km

Locations: Orel, Livny, Kursk, Belgorod, Voronezh, Kharkov, Izyum, Dnepropetrovsk, Don, Donets, Dnepr, Stalingrad, Rostov, Kotelnikovo, Volga, Perekop, Sea of Azov, Elista, Kerch, Sevastopol, Novorossiysk, Maykop, Yalta, Grozny, Black Sea, Caspian Sea

ROMANIANS ON THE EASTERN FRONT

Romanian troops played a small part in Operation Barbarossa in 1941. The head of government, Marshal Ion Antonescu, saw this as part of a holy crusade against Bolshevism and agreed to increase the Romanian force in 1942. When the Soviets smashed the Axis defences around Stalingrad, over 100,000 Romanians were killed or captured. Even so, strong Romanian forces would continue to fight alongside the Germans until August 1944, when their country changed sides after a coup led by King Michael deposed Antonescu. Substantial Romanian forces then advanced with the Red Army into Hungary and Czechoslovakia.

Above: Romanian prisoners near Stalingrad, late 1942.

to escape through Rostov by the end of January, but the slower-moving infantry of Seventeenth Army were pushed east into a bridgehead in the Taman Peninsula opposite the Crimea.

The Soviet commanders now had new objectives in their sights. On the northern flank they would push forward to both Kursk and Kharkov, and to the south they would cross the Donets and head for the Dniepr to isolate Manstein's forces. These attacks began in the last days of January.

The Soviets also planned to strengthen these attacks by switching the troops that had finally captured Stalingrad to the main battlefront. However, this move took longer than was originally planned.

LAST ADVANCES

Soviet advances did capture Kursk and Rostov in early February and were moving past Kharkov by the middle of the month, but the troops were becoming increasingly worn out. In mid-February Hitler re-organized his forces, putting Manstein, his most able general of all, in charge of what would now be called Army Group South. The great Russian advances had created a number of exposed salients at the same time, because the German retreat had shortened their lines. All this added up to an opportunity for a German riposte, which would begin in mid-February.

Below: Red Army infantry attack. Riflemen advance while a light machine-gun gives covering fire.

Below: Soviet troops often went into action riding on tanks, a practice that risked high casualties.

Propaganda, Art and Popular Culture

Since WWII was indeed a total war, writers, artists, movie-makers, journalists and broadcasters everywhere played their parts in the war effort, either within the dictates of totalitarian rulers or under the gentler controls imposed in the democracies.

In the totalitarian nations, art, entertainment and public information were simply aspects of national life to be managed for the good of the state, whether in war or in peace. The situation was less clear-cut in the democracies, but generally speaking popular and more serious artists and those in the media felt an obligation to make some contribution to their respective war efforts.

ABSOLUTE CONTROL

There were many similarities between the situation in the USSR and Germany and even Japan. In all three countries censorship was absolute; nothing was published or broadcast

Below: *Signal* magazine was issued by the Germans in several languages. This French example publicized the Katyń massacre.

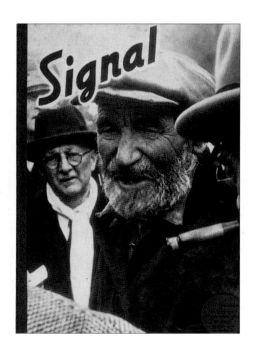

that had not been officially approved, nor was any criticism of the ruling regime tolerated. The Nazis were particularly aware of the power of radio broadcasting. They ensured that cheap radio sets were widely available in Germany but confiscated many radios in occupied countries, banning anyone under their control from listening to Allied broadcasts.

In the visual arts there were also many similarities between the socialist realism style demanded by Soviet authorities and the classicism favoured by Hitler and the Nazis. The stern Aryan soldiers of German war art were little different from the undaunted workers and peasants their opponents depicted.

German and Soviet portrayals of their opponents were nasty in the extreme. The Nazi demonization of communists and Jews needs no elaboration, while on the Soviet side well-known and much-publicized material included poems entitled "Kill Him" and "I Hate".

Depictions of the Axis powers in Britain and the USA were neither as crude nor as vicious, though some well-known wartime films, *The Life and Death of Colonel Blimp* for example, were criticized in some quarters for including characters who were decent Germans. One thing that almost all belligerent nations on both sides had in common was that newspaper circulations increased substantially, though

JOSEF GOEBBELS

Goebbels (1897–1945) was the Nazi Propaganda Minister from Hitler's accession to power in 1933 until, after murdering their six children, he and his wife committed suicide in Hitler's bunker in April 1945. He controlled all the media and artistic output in Germany. He used radio broadcasting particularly brilliantly to foster support for the Nazi regime and to create and maintain the image of Hitler as a great leader. He was loyal to Hitler to the end and his efforts played a large part in keeping the German people fighting effectively long after defeat was certain.

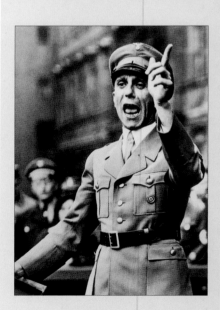

Above: Josef Goebbels in full oratorical flow at a Nazi Party rally in 1934.

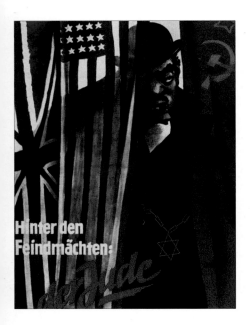

Above: "Behind the enemy powers: the Jew", a German poster of 1942.

in most countries the number of different publications decreased, while the survivors were reduced by paper rationing to a handful of pages.

BROADCAST MEDIA

In Britain and the USA, owners and managers of the press and broadcast media were happy generally to comply with official wishes that they gave no secrets to the enemy and to moderate any criticisms of the government that they might have. But neither government sought to dictate what was printed or broadcast and certainly did not disseminate the sort of outright lies that were a commonplace of Nazi bulletins.

Many in Europe secretly listened to the BBC, in part because they knew that its news was truthful as far as it went, even if it was not always the whole truth. But Germany's English-language broadcasts

Right: Laurence Olivier as the king in his 1944 film, *Henry V*.

were mocked in Britain for the stilted style of the principal broadcaster William Joyce (known as "Lord Haw-Haw") and the ludicrous stories he often tried to tell his listeners.

Film was probably the most powerful cultural medium. As well as productions on topical subjects, the output both from Hollywood and the state-run German film industry included much simple escapist entertainment for difficult times. Historical epics featuring past patriots and heroes appeared regularly in Germany and the USSR – *Bismarck* and *Ivan the Terrible* among the titles – and in Britain Laurence Olivier's 1944 version of Shakespeare's *Henry V* had a similar theme.

For many, popular music and song were a source of comfort and pleasure that could transcend boundaries. At the end of the African campaign in 1943 there was an incident in which a

Above: Underground newspapers, like France's communist *l'Humanité*, provided an alternative source of news in every occupied country.

formation of British soldiers, marching to their victory parade in Tunis, passed a column from the *Afrika Korps* going into captivity – both groups were singing "Lili Marlene".

Alamein and the Advance to Tunisia

*Although it could not compare in scale to the massive battles on the Eastern Front,
El Alamein is rightly seen as a turning point in Britain's war with Germany.
Much hard fighting remained but after Alamein there would be no more big defeats.*

Although his charge into Egypt had been halted in the First Battle of El Alamein in July 1942, Rommel was keen to attack again as soon as his forces were strengthened. In the meantime, Prime Minister Churchill had appointed a new command team to the British forces defending Egypt, putting General Bernard Montgomery in charge of Eighth Army.

NEW BRITISH PLANS

As soon as he took over, "Monty" began transforming the British force, beginning by rebuilding its morale, which had been shattered by the disasters earlier in the year. He laid down far more clearly than before that there would be no retreat and deployed his forces to make best use of their concentrated firepower, rather than try to

NORTH AFRICA, 1942–3 After victory at El Alamein and the Torch landings, the Allied forces steadily completed their African victory.

KEY FACTS – EL ALAMEIN

PLACE: North-west Egypt

DATE: 23 October–4 November 1942

OUTCOME: Italian and German forces defeated and forced to retreat to western Libya.

Above: A Crusader Mark 3 tank during the Battle of El Alamein. Some 4,500 of all versions of the Crusader were built, but all were mechanically unreliable.

---

compete with the Germans in manoeuvre. Thus, when the Germans attacked late on 30 August, the British units stood firm and by 6 September the Germans had been forced back to where they had started from. This Battle of Alam Halfa was a clear Allied victory.

A significant factor in the German defeat was their shortage of supplies. They were operating many hundreds of kilometres from their nearest port, while the routes between Europe and North Africa were coming under increasingly heavy Allied air and naval attacks. Many of these raids were coming from the island of Malta, very heavily bombarded earlier in the year but by now reinforced after a series of fierce naval convoy battles.

After Alam Halfa, Churchill wanted Montgomery to attack straight away but he refused, insisting that he be allowed to build up his forces substantially first. By the time he did attack

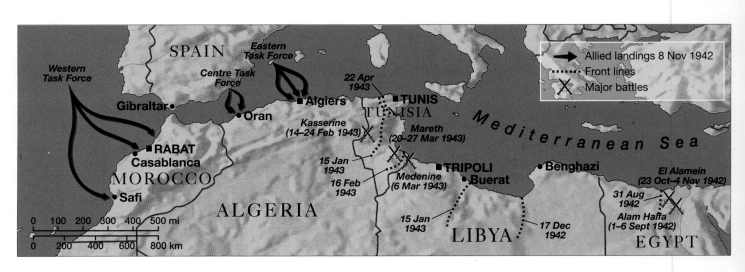

Right: A British 5.5in (140mm) gun firing during the heavy bombardment that opened the El Alamein battle.

at El Alamein in October, Eighth Army had about a two to one superiority in men, tanks and guns and a considerable advantage in the air (and much of the Axis force was made up of less effective Italian units).

Rommel had built up a formidable position by using extensive minefields and other defences, but Montgomery had trained his troops meticulously. He made certain that his infantry, tank units and artillery worked together effectively, which had seldom happened in the previous desert battles.

ALAMEIN VICTORY

Several days of attritional fighting followed the initial Allied advance. Gradually, the German tank units, which provided the backbone of the Axis defences, were worn away. On 2 November Rommel signalled to Hitler that he had to retreat. Hitler responded with his usual unrealistic "no retreat" order, but it made no difference. With only a couple of dozen of the 500 tanks with which he began the battle left in action, Rommel

Below: Italian troops run for cover under Allied air attack in the early stages of the Battle of El Alamein.

had no alternative. On 4 November he abandoned his whole defensive position.

Partly because Montgomery did not organize an energetic enough pursuit, much of the remaining Axis force got away. A long retreat followed, made even more necessary for Rommel this time because of the Anglo-American Torch landings in north-west Africa from 8 November.

After brief pauses to allow supplies to catch up, Eighth Army captured Tripoli on 23 January 1943, after an advance of some 1,500km (930 miles). Despite German demolitions, the British were able to begin using the port facilities to some extent by the end of the month.

It would be several weeks before the leading troops could be strengthened for further substantial advances, but they did manage to push forward to Medenine, in eastern Tunisia, in early February.

FIELD MARSHAL BERNARD MONTGOMERY

Montgomery (1887–1976) was Britain's most famous general of the war. His careful planning and methodical leadership played a large part in the succession of Allied victories in North Africa, Italy and north-west Europe from autumn 1942 to the end of the war. In particular, it is unlikely that D-Day would have gone so well without his contribution to the planning process. However, some historians believe that he was over-cautious and thereby lost opportunities for cheaper and quicker victories.

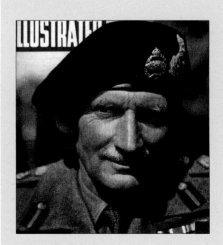

Above: "Monty" showing off his trademark pair of cap badges.

Operation Torch and Victory in Africa

American troops made their combat debut in the European theatre in Operation Torch in 1942. After setbacks and much hard fighting, the Allied victory in North Africa was completed in May 1943, as the ring around Germany began to tighten.

From early 1941 US policy in the event of war with Germany and Japan was to give the European theatre priority. From the start US Army leaders were convinced that the way to defeat Hitler was by a cross-Channel attack from England, but it was very soon obvious that this operation could not be mounted for many months. To maintain the "Germany first" policy President Roosevelt ordered that US troops must be sent into battle against Germany during 1942, so it was decided to make landings in Morocco and Algeria to clear North Africa of Axis forces.

Morocco and Algeria were French colonies under the control of Marshal Pétain's Vichy

Below: An American M2 105mm (4.13in) howitzer position in southern Tunisia in the spring of 1943.

regime. Anglo-French relations remained embittered after the events of 1940 so the Americans took the lead in pre-landing negotiations to try to persuade the leaders of the large Vichy forces in Africa not to resist the Allied advance and, instead, join with the smaller Free French forces already fighting on the Allied side. In the event the French did not resist the land-

ings strongly, but it took months of political wrangling to create a united Free French force.

TORCH LANDINGS

The invasion, known as Operation Torch, began on 8 November 1942, four days after Eighth Army's victory at El Alamein had sent the Italians and Germans reeling out of Egypt. Ideally the attack would have gone as far east as Tunisia, but this was rejected as too risky. Instead landings were made on Morocco's Atlantic coast near Casablanca and around Algiers and Oran in Algeria. The Anglo-American force, First Army, immediately began heading east for Tunis, but too little too late.

Field Marshal Albrecht Kesselring, Germany's very able Commander-in-Chief South, started pouring troops, tanks and aircraft into Tunisia from Sicily on 9 November. These fought the Allied advance to a standstill in the rugged hills of western Tunisia, in a series of bitter battles from late November into early January 1943.

BATTLE FOR TUNISIA

By February 1943 the Axis forces in Tunisia had been joined by Rommel's army, which had successfully completed its retreat from Egypt. Eighth Army was still struggling to bring the port of Tripoli into full use so was not yet ready to push farther into Tunisia in the south. This gave

Above: American troops landing at Oran with a light anti-aircraft gun at the start of Operation Torch.

In April First and Eighth Armies continued their attacks. They eventually broke out of the hills and advanced to Bizerta and Tunis in early May. The last of around 250,000 Axis troops taken prisoner in these final battles surrendered on 13 May. Africa was now wholly in Allied hands.

the Germans an opportunity to strike at First Army, which they took on 14 February.

In the resulting Battle of Kasserine the inexperienced American troops, who were the initial target for the attack, were badly defeated. American and British reinforcements, rushed to the threatened sector, just prevented a decisive breakthrough and then gradually recovered much of the lost ground by late February. General George Patton took over command of the US ground forces in Tunisia and his leadership very quickly improved their combat efficiency.

In early March Eighth Army smashed an attempted German attack and later in the month, in the hard-fought Battle of Mareth, pushed the Axis forces out of their main defence line in southern Tunisia.

Below: US troops examining an abandoned Italian M13/40 tank during the fighting in Tunisia.

GENERAL DWIGHT D. EISENHOWER

Eisenhower (1890–1969) was appointed as Allied supreme commander for Operation Torch and would continue in that role in Sicily and Italy and then finally in north-west Europe in 1944–5. He realized far better than other top Allied commanders the paramount importance of maintaining good relations within the Anglo-American partnership. Although he had numerous problems with egotistical subordinates like Patton and Montgomery, Eisenhower's leadership kept the Allied effort very much on track.

Above: Eisenhower was totally committed to Allied unity.

Germany Fights Back: Kharkov and Kursk

The counter-stroke at Kharkov inspired Hitler to order new attacks at Kursk. For the first time a major German summer offensive in Russia failed to break through, a clear sign that the Soviets were now winning their Great Patriotic War.

The Soviet advances during January and February 1943 had pushed deep into German-held territory to capture the city of Kharkov and threaten Dnepropetrovsk. To the north of this penetration the German Army Group Centre was holding firm around Orel, and to the south General Manstein's Army Group South had good defensive positions along the Mius River. Manstein now had several Panzer divisions available, including strong and well-equipped Waffen-SS units. He

---

KEY FACTS – KURSK

PLACE: Between Orel and Kharkov, Eastern Front

DATE: 4–13 July 1943

OUTCOME: German forces failed to break through in the biggest tank battle of the war.

Below: German troops fighting on the outskirts of Kharkov at the end of February 1943.

was ready to turn the tables on the Soviet attackers in between these bastions.

BATTLE OF KHARKOV
In the second half of February Manstein's tank units struck against the Soviet spearheads near Dnepropetrovsk. By the end of the month four Soviet tank and mechanized corps (each roughly equivalent to a German Panzer division) had been smashed and the survivors pushed back over the Donets.

Taking advantage of the last few days of firm frozen ground before the mud of the spring thaw, Manstein's tanks next headed for Kharkov, taking it by 16 March. Hitler was so heartened by this remarkable comeback that, even before Kharkov fell, he was issuing orders for a new attack against the large Soviet salient centred around Kursk to the north.

OPERATION CITADEL
Although the Germans had lost perhaps half a million casualties over the winter, Hitler still believed he could regain the initiative on the Eastern Front and, at the same time, make provision in western and southern Europe for whatever the Anglo-Americans might attempt during the year. It was clear that the German troops, and especially their tank forces, were still usually more skilled in combat than the Red Army. Hitler also believed that new Tiger and

Panther tanks coming into service would give them a further qualitative edge.

The German plan was for Ninth Army from Field Marshal Günther von Kluge's Army Group Centre to attack the north flank of the salient, while Fourth Panzer Army from Manstein's Army Group South drove into the southern flank. Originally Hitler planned the advance to begin in May, but he repeatedly postponed it until more of the new tanks were ready.

For their part Stalin, Zhukov and Chief of the General Staff Marshal Aleksandr Vasilevsky (in effect the command team who would run the remainder of the Soviet Union's war) decided to stand on the defensive at first, while they also prepared offensives of their own north and south of Kursk. Through spies and other intelligence the Soviets had a reasonable idea of what the Germans planned and accordingly they massively re-inforced their defences in the threatened areas.

The German advances began on 4 July and were fiercely resisted from the start. In the north

Ninth Army, with seven Panzer divisions leading its attack, made a little progress at first. The Soviet commanders then committed their tank reserves. On 9 July Kluge told Hitler that he could not break through. On the 12th the Soviets began their offensive north of Orel and Kluge had to retreat.

On the southern front things seemed to go better for the Germans. Fourth Panzer Army advanced about 35km (20 miles) in the first few days, losing heavily but inflicting more casualties than it received. On the 12th there was a giant tank

Above: German Panzer 4 tanks advancing across open ground during the Battle of Kursk.

battle near the small town of Prokhorovka. Again, though the Soviets probably came off worse, they had outnumbered the Germans from the start and could afford to do so.

On the 13 July, with no breakthrough in sight and the Anglo-American invasion of Sicily developing, Hitler called off further attacks. With that, the initiative on the Eastern Front finally and permanently passed to the Red Army.

FIELD MARSHAL ERICH VON MANSTEIN

The most talented general of any country during WWII was Germany's Field Marshal von Manstein (1887–1973). He was very largely responsible for the brilliantly successful German plan for attacking France in 1940. Although he failed in the attempt to relieve Stalingrad in late 1942, his leadership over the following months stabilized the Eastern Front and led to the German success at Kharkov. At Kursk his attacks were the most successful part of the German offensive. Thereafter, Manstein fought resourcefully on the retreat until Hitler dismissed him in March 1944.

Right: Field Marshal von Manstein and his staff studying a map to plan their manoeuvres.

Codes and Code Breaking

The continuous struggle to read enemy messages was an ongoing aspect of every campaign of the war. Signals intelligence contributed to many victories but was probably not the war-winning advantage that is sometimes suggested.

All the major combatants in WWII put considerable effort into reading coded enemy radio messages. Overall, Britain and the USA had the most success and made the best use of the resulting information; the USA and USSR were the most successful in keeping their own messages secure (though even now little is publicly known of Soviet efforts in this field).

CIPHER SYSTEMS

Encryption methods used in WWII included manual systems (based on printed sets of random numbers) and machines, which were more complex and theoretically more secure. Signals produced on some machines are thought never to have been broken. These included the American Sigaba type and the British Typex. Less secure machines included the German Enigma and Geheimschreiber, the Japanese diplomatic service machine known to the Allies as Purple, and the American M-209 (used for low-grade traffic). Efforts to decode messages led to the development in Britain and the USA of various forms of calculating equipment, including what are now regarded as the first electronic computers.

Britain had various successes, increasingly comprehensive as the war went on, against German and Italian systems. For their part the Axis powers were able to read many Royal Navy messages up to 1943.

BREAKING ENIGMA

The British system built on prewar French and Polish work. The first messages decoded were from the general Luftwaffe Enigma cipher in May 1940 and then other breaks followed. The process was by no means continuous. The main U-boat cipher was broken for much of 1941 but was impenetrable for most of 1942, both times with important

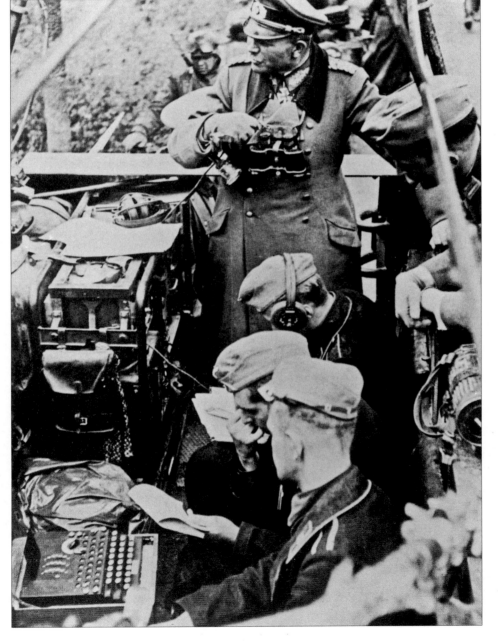

Left: An Enigma machine (bottom left) in use on General Guderian's command vehicle in 1940.

Above: Alan Turing, one of the leading mathematicians in the British code-breaking organization.

effects in the Battle of the Atlantic. One of the strengths of the British set-up was its centralization at the Government Code and Cypher School at Bletchley Park, where the various departments worked together well, enhancing each other's techniques and sharing information.

By contrast Germany, Italy and Japan all had a range of agencies involved in this work and these often competed with each other. And even when information was shared between services or with Axis partners, its

Below: *U-505* alongside the USS *Pillsbury*. This 1944 capture was based on code-breaking information.

Right: General Oshima (left), Japan's ambassador in Berlin, whose messages home were decoded by the Allies.

recipients did not necessarily trust it – the Italians warned the Germans about Allied code breaking and the Germans warned the Japanese, in both cases with little effect.

The German Navy's B-Dienst had good results with the main Royal Navy operational ciphers at various periods up to 1943 and systems used by Allied merchant ships into 1944. From late 1943 the manual systems were replaced in Royal Navy service by the highly secure Typex machine already used by the other British services.

In the Pacific the American-led Allied effort had great success first with the Japanese diplomatic cipher, then with the Japanese Navy and finally the Army systems. Curiously, among the most valuable results was the insight given into German plans. Japan's diplomats in Berlin and elsewhere sent extensive reports on new German weapons and defences, which were read by the Allies.

The breaking of the Japanese Navy's JN-25 cipher made a major contribution to the US victory at Midway that turned the tide of the Pacific War.

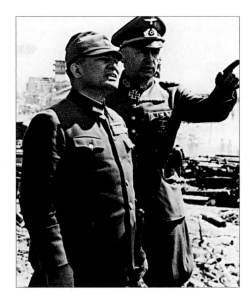

Later code-breaking information helped Allied commanders decide which garrisons to attack and which to bypass. However, it is not true (as has sometimes been suggested) that properly interpreted Purple and JN-25 decrypts made by the US, British or Dutch services could have given definite warning of Japan's attack on Pearl Harbor.

GARDENING

During their normal operations RAF bombers often dropped sea mines near German-controlled ports. This activity was known by the codename "gardening". This was not just done to sink enemy ships, however. Many such operations were meant to be detected by the Germans so that their local HQ would send a warning to its units. Allied cryptographers then used the predictable content of such signals to work out the code-machine settings for the day – and then they would use these settings to read more important messages.

The Defeat of Hitler's Navy, 1942–5

The struggle against Germany's U-boats continued to 1945 but was decisively won in the spring of 1943 by a combination of airpower, scientific research, code-breaking skill, industrial strength – and the bravery of the Allied seamen.

By the end of 1941 the battles between Germany's U-boats and the Allied merchant ships and escorts had already been raging bitterly for many months. Though the threat was serious, Britain was surviving reasonably well. Rationing had reduced consumption substantially and new construction, and the transfer to British control of ships from occupied Allied countries like Norway and Greece, had helped to counter-act losses. However, Hitler's declaration of war on the USA in December 1941 brought new opportunities, which his U-boat force soon grabbed.

For the first six months or so of 1942 the U-boats scored many successes off the US East

Above: A British heavy cruiser in service with an Arctic convoy to Russia in early 1943.

Coast and in the Caribbean. The main reason for this was an astounding failure on the part of American commanders to institute a system of escorted convoys and supporting air units. Convoys linking with those on the trans-Atlantic routes were gradually introduced from April but did not cover the whole area to the Gulf of Mexico until October. Although the situation was thus being brought under control by the summer, the Allied shipping losses of June 1942 were the worst of the war.

GERMAN ADVANTAGES

On the German side matters were helped by code changes that shut the British crypto-graphers out of the main U-boat traffic from February 1942 to the end of the year. The size of the U-boat force was also increasing from some 100 opera-tional boats in January 1942 to

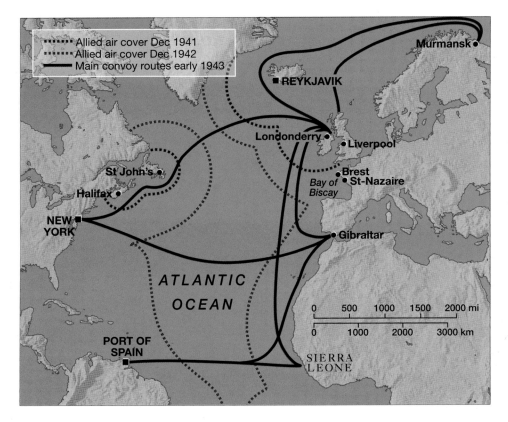

Allied air cover Dec 1941
Allied air cover Dec 1942
Main convoy routes early 1943

Murmansk
REYKJAVIK
Londonderry
Liverpool
St John's
Brest
St-Nazaire
Bay of Biscay
Halifax
NEW YORK
Gibraltar
ATLANTIC OCEAN
PORT OF SPAIN
SIERRA LEONE

| 0 | 500 | 1000 | 1500 | 2000 mi |
| 0 | 1000 | 2000 | 3000 km |

BATTLE OF THE ATLANTIC
Convoy routes and air cover areas at the height of the battle.

over 200 a year later. Ultimately, though, they were fighting a losing battle in the production race. July 1942 was the first month of the war when new ships launched on the Allied side exceeded losses, and the American shipbuilding effort was still expanding rapidly.

Although the point was past when there was any likelihood of Germany winning the Battle of the Atlantic, a further crisis was to come. This was caused by poor allocation of resources on the Allied side. Although shipping losses were delaying the US build-up in Britain, and hence the subsequent invasion of north-west Europe that was supposed to be the principal Allied plan, the forces allocated to the Atlantic battle were relatively weak. This was especially true in the vital category of very long-range aircraft, with hundreds being used by the heavy bomber forces in England and the US Navy in the

Above: The merchant ship *Pennsylvania Sun* burning after an attack by *U-571* in July 1942.

Pacific but, until well into 1943, only a handful being allocated to the convoy routes.

CLIMAX OF THE BATTLE

In a series of frantic convoy battles in March 1943 the U-boats scored their last significant victories, sinking about a fifth of the ships crossing the Atlantic at that time with very little loss to themselves. Within weeks, however, the situation was transformed. In May, 41 U-boats were sunk, and Admiral Dönitz abandoned his tactic of pack attacks on convoys.

There were many reasons for this sudden change. More Allied aircraft were committed to the battle, both ship-borne in escort carriers and land-based. Allied ship and airborne radars were much improved, as were anti-submarine weapons. Tactics and training of escort ships were much more sophisticated. And, by no means least, the British code breakers were again reliably reading German messages.

The Allies would hold their lead in all these categories until the war's end, despite German efforts to turn the tide with new

weapons and tactics. Although numerous U-boats remained in action until May 1945 (and they still achieved a few scattered sinkings), by the final months most new U-boats were being sunk before they finished their first war patrols.

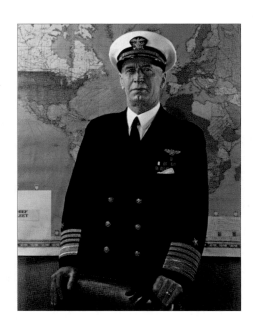

Above: Admiral Ernest King was the highly effective head of the US Navy 1942–5 but was slow to set up the convoy system off the US coast.

ADMIRAL KARL DÖNITZ

Dönitz (1891–1980) was the head of the German submarine service from the start of the war and Commander-in-Chief of the German Navy from January 1943. When Hitler committed suicide in 1945, Dönitz briefly became his successor. Dönitz had been a U-boat captain in WWI and commanded the U-boat force very resourcefully throughout WWII. Dönitz thought his U-boats could win the war for Germany, but too few were built to achieve this until far too late.

Allied Grand Strategy

Britain and the USA never agreed a formal alliance treaty during WWII but, despite this and their radically different political systems and ways of life, they generally co-operated effectively to defeat Germany.

Throughout the war there were a number of summit meetings between Churchill and Roosevelt and their top advisers. Sometimes these also involved other Allied leaders like the French and Chinese. There were also three summit meetings with Stalin, and Churchill travelled separately to Moscow during 1942.

MILITARY PLANS

More important in the very close and generally amicable Anglo-American co-operation that developed was the creation of an integrated military planning system. Britain and the USA both had chiefs of staff committees of their top soldiers, sailors and airmen to oversee their national military operations. However, a new body, the Combined Chiefs of Staff,

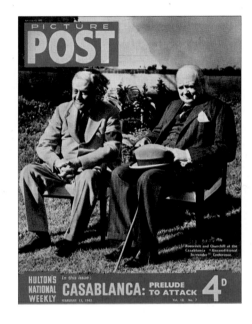

Above: Roosevelt and Churchill seen in contemporary coverage of the Casablanca Conference.

Below: Churchill and his Chiefs of Staff in 1945. Front row from left, Air Marshal Portal, General Brooke, Churchill, Admiral Cunningham.

was created by the first inter-Allied conference after the USA joined the war: the Washington "Arcadia" conference during December 1940–January 1941.

The Combined Chiefs normally met in Washington and included the US Joint Chiefs in person and representatives of the British Chiefs permanently assigned to this duty. This body agreed many of the vital details of major military plans and allocated resources accordingly.

At a lower level all major Anglo-American operations in the European theatre, from the D-Day invasion down, were planned and staffed by fully integrated command teams. One of the most notable achievements of General Eisenhower, as Allied Supreme Commander for a number of European operations, was to ensure that disagreements along national lines were avoided as much as possible.

The summits also included meetings of the Combined Chiefs (though in this case the British Chiefs of Staff would be personally present) and here national disagreements were perhaps inevitably more common. There were two Allied conferences at Quebec, a second one at Washington, and one each at Casablanca, Cairo and Malta. Each had complicated discussions and arguments that cannot be outlined in detail here. However, certain important themes can be highlighted.

CROSS-CHANNEL ATTACK

The American leaders consistently believed that the best way to defeat Germany was the most direct: build up forces in Britain, invade across the Channel and head straight to Berlin. From bitter experience the British were all too well aware of the fighting power of the German Army. They were unwilling to risk a major defeat by a premature cross-Channel invasion. They also believed that too single-minded a concentration on this one objective would be to neglect important interests in the Mediterranean and prevent the Allies responding successfully to opportunities that might arise.

Generally speaking the British were more successful in getting their views adopted as policy in 1942–3, when their war effort was still more substantial than the USA's, than in the later period when the USA's strength was still expanding as Britain's declined. In practice this meant that the clearance of North Africa and the subsequent invasion of Sicily and southern Italy in 1942–3 were not originally welcomed by the American Chiefs and that the later removal of many resources from the Italian campaign was bitterly opposed by the British.

The summits with Stalin (in Teheran, Yalta and Potsdam, at the last of which Harry Truman and Clement Attlee replaced Roosevelt and Churchill) were more about how post-war Europe should be organized

than about agreeing military plans. Ultimately, one truth became plain: the war would end with the Red Army in control across eastern Europe and Stalin would rule it as he saw fit, whatever wartime promises he might make regarding free elections and similar matters.

Above: Stalin, Roosevelt and Churchill during their first conference at Teheran in 1943.

However, Stalin did keep his promise, made at Teheran in November 1943, to join the war against Japan shortly after the end of the war in Europe.

Right: Managing shipping, like these newly launched American Liberty ships, was a key aspect of Anglo-American co-operation.

Sicily and Italy, 1943–4

The Allied invasion of Sicily in July 1943 was followed by landings in mainland Italy in September. These knocked Italy out of the war, but the German Army's continued stubborn defence meant that there would be no rapid Allied victory.

In their meeting at Casablanca at the start of 1943, the Anglo-American leaders decided to invade Sicily as soon as possible after the campaign in North Africa was over. Accordingly, Operation Husky began on 10 July 1943. The preparations for the operation were bedevilled by many changes of plan in which the overall ground commander, General Harold Alexander, proved unable to direct his principal subordinates: General Montgomery, commanding British Eighth Army, and General Patton, commanding US Seventh Army. As a result, there was never a clear plan for the capture of the island, and opportunities to win the battle quickly and decisively were missed.

Although many of the accompanying airborne troops landed in the sea and drowned because of poor pilot training and bad weather, the initial Allied landings in the south and south-east of Sicily were a success. The large Italian forces put up little resistance and many surrendered readily – however, the German troops were a different matter. They used the rugged terrain expertly in a series of delaying actions, while the Allied commanders quarrelled over how to conduct the campaign. Finally the Germans withdrew across the Straits of Messina in mid-August virtually unmolested by the superior Allied air and naval forces.

AFTER SICILY

With so many troops and resources committed to the Mediterranean by early 1943, and no possibility of organizing a cross-Channel invasion before 1944, the Allied leaders faced a dilemma. Britain wanted to continue Mediterranean operations and, since the alternative was to have the troops stand idle, the Americans agreed in May 1943 that an invasion of mainland Italy would follow the battles

ITALY, 1943–5

Throughout the campaign in Sicily and Italy the Allied forces had to fight hard for every advance.

for Sicily. Once again there were disputes about planning and priorities that would continue to affect the Italian campaign to the end of the war.

Mussolini had been deposed as head of the Italian government in July and the new regime began secret peace talks with the Allies. On 3 September Eighth Army crossed from Sicily to the toe of Italy and on the 8th the Italian surrender was announced. The Germans were ready, however, and had moved reinforcements into the country to take over. On the 9th the main Allied landings, by General Mark Clark's US Fifth Army, went in around Salerno, just south of Naples, and were nearly thrown back into the sea during the first few days.

SLOW RETREAT

For the rest of the year the Germans fell back slowly from one well-defended river line to the next. Eighth Army pushed up the east side of Italy and Fifth Army to the west. By the turn of the year the Allied advance had reached the Germans' Gustav Line, whose

Below: German paratroops bring supplies to the Cassino defences.

Above: A US cargo ship explodes off a Sicilian beach following a German air attack, July 1943.

most famous bastion was centred on Monte Cassino, still well to the south of Rome.

In an attempt to break the stalemate the Allied forces made an amphibious landing at Anzio, behind the German lines, on 22 January 1944. The troops there, timidly led, soon found themselves effectively besieged in their beachhead. Repeated attacks on the Gustav Line over the following months also failed.

During May 1944 the Allies at last mounted a properly co-ordinated attack all along the Italian front, and this time they captured Cassino and broke the Gustav Line. By then, however, Montgomery and many veteran troops had left to prepare for D-Day and Italy had slipped down the Allied priority list. Rome fell on 4 June, but by autumn 1944 the Germans were again making a stand, this time on the Gothic Line just north of Florence.

Below: A British Bofors gun in the ruins below Monte Cassino.

Night Bombing of Germany, 1939–44

After the French surrender, aerial attack was the only way in which Britain could strike back directly at Germany. RAF leaders welcomed the development of an all-out bombing campaign; they thought that their service could win the war on its own.

Britain's Royal Air Force (RAF) had been created in 1918 specifically to bomb Germany and held to this aim as war approached in the 1930s. A small number of daylight raids during the Phoney War showed that bombers were hopelessly vulnerable to fighter attack and confirmed that, when attacks began in earnest in 1940, they would be made mainly at night.

In the first phase, up to early 1942, very little was achieved, though losses, compared to some later points in the campaign, were also modest. Bombers were sent to attack specific targets – individual factories or rail junctions, for example – but in fact their navigational skills were so poor that they rarely hit them.

AREA BOMBING

Air Marshal "Bomber" Harris took over at the head of RAF Bomber Command in early 1942 and changed tactics, at that

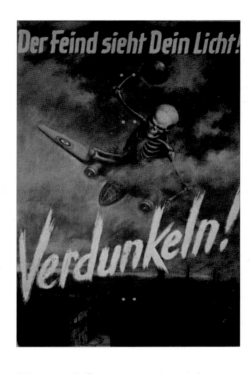

Above: A German poster urging blackout precautions.

stage with full support from his service and political superiors. Throughout his period in command Harris believed that "area bombing" of the residential districts of enemy cities was the

only sensible use of his force and that, correctly applied, it would win the war.

The aim was to cripple the German war effort by attacking the morale of the working population, killing some and at least dehousing many others. Little thought was given to whether this was a morally justifiable means of waging war.

The first effective attacks in this vein came in the late spring of 1942, most notably a handful of "thousand-bomber" raids that employed all of Bomber Command's training aircraft, as well as the operational force. These raids coincided with the introduction of Gee, the first significant electronic navigation aid, and the beginning of a process whereby the accuracy of attacks was improved. However, Harris foolishly opposed the creation of a Pathfinder Force to lead attacks and mark targets but he was overruled.

Throughout 1942 the aircraft used by Bomber Command also greatly improved, with the four-engined Halifax and Lancaster types with their large bomb loads predominating by early 1943. Thus, the roughly 5,000 bomber sorties flown in June 1942 dropped 6,950 tonnes of bombs. However, only a year later in June 1943, the 5,800 bomber sorties flown dropped well over 15,500 tonnes.

Left: A classic image of a Lancaster bomber setting off on a mission.

Above: A Lancaster bomber over Hamburg, silhouetted by flares and ground fires in a time-exposure photo taken from another bomber.

In response to these increasingly damaging attacks the Germans built up a formidable night-fighter force and control system. Initially this relied exclusively on ground stations directing twin-engined heavy fighter designs into close enough contact with a target aircraft that their radar systems could complete the interception. Later single-engined day fighters were sent by radio to the skies above the cities being attacked and were able to make visual interceptions.

In response the RAF concentrated its aircraft to swamp particular sectors of the system, as well as jamming radars and using electronic and other deception measures to fool controllers or blind their equipment.

In 1943 Bomber Command devastated many cities across Germany, but the only time it came close to achieving the sort of results Harris expected was in a series of attacks on Hamburg in July. These benefited from a temporary Allied advantage in the electronic warfare struggle and because of this and other special circumstances were never to be repeated.

BATTLE OF BERLIN
In the winter of 1943–4 Harris mounted what he called the Battle of Berlin. However, for all the damage inflicted, this series of attacks on the German capital and other cities was ultimately a defeat for Bomber Command. Losses rose to a rate that could

AIR MARSHAL ARTHUR HARRIS

Harris (1892–1984) led RAF Bomber Command from February 1942 to the end of the war. Harris fervently believed that, suitably strengthened, his command could win the war on its own by bombing Germany's cities. His leadership undoubtedly transformed the morale and effectiveness of Bomber Command, which were at a very low ebb when he took over. However, his forces lost increasingly heavily in 1943–4 and only their partial diversion to support operations in France saved them from an even greater defeat.

Above: Air Marshal Harris (seated) and senior members of his staff at Bomber Command.

not have been sustained for long, while the German economy and civilian morale never came close to collapse. Though Harris complained bitterly and disobeyed his orders as much as possible, it was a respite for Bomber Command to be switched partly to targets in France over the next months, in preparation for D-Day.

US Strategic Bombing, 1942–3

Formations of American Flying Fortress and Liberator bombers began ranging over Europe in mid-1942. Their leaders hoped to bring the Luftwaffe and the German economy to their knees, but their initial efforts were bloodily defeated.

Like Britain's RAF, the United States Army Air Force (USAAF) entered the war committed to a policy of long-range strategic bombing. Like the RAF in 1939, it believed in making daylight attacks on precise targets, relying on the heavy defensive armament of its bomber aircraft and their tight formations to ward off enemy fighters. Like the RAF it would also discover that bombing accuracy never approached the anticipated results and that bomber formations could not defend themselves adequately against fighter attack.

The principal USAAF heavy-bomber organization throughout the campaign was the Eighth Air Force (AF), based in Britain. The Ninth and Twelfth AF, based in North Africa in 1942–3, also included heavy-bomber units, which were transferred to

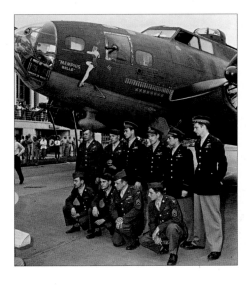

Above: B-17 *Memphis Belle* and its crew on their return Stateside after completing their 25-mission tour of duty, one of the first crews to do so.

the Fifteenth AF, operational in southern Italy from the end of October 1943.

The first raid over western Europe by a wholly American bomber force was on 17 August 1942 against targets at Rouen in northern France. For the remainder of that year all targets attacked were similarly short-range and the bomber forces were provided with strong fighter escorts, both from the RAF and the American forces. The build-up of the American bomber strength was slow. By the end of the year only some 1,550 sorties had been flown, with 32 aircraft lost.

ATTACKING GERMANY

The first raid on a German target was against Wilhelmshaven on 27 January 1943; 91 aircraft attacked, with 3 shot down in return for 6 German fighters. This would prove to be an unusually favourable ratio of losses for the Americans.

For the next several months other German ports were also targeted along with French ports used as U-boat bases. The raids on the French ports, like those conducted by the RAF in the same period, were a fiasco. They flattened the homes of the local French population but barely scratched the thick concrete of the U-boat pens.

Eighth AF first flew over 2,000 sorties in June 1943 and would pass the 6,000 mark monthly in January 1944. The attacks by the British-based

Left: A B-24 Liberator on fire after being hit by flak. Watching comrades die like this was difficult, to say the least, for bomber crews.

Above: A formation of B-17s on a raid over Germany. Bombing accuracy in cloudy European skies never matched expectations.

Above: Bombs dropping away from a B-17 during a raid on Bremen. Other attacking aircraft leave condensation trails below.

forces were joined, from the early summer of 1943, by raids on targets in Italy and elsewhere from North Africa.

Although the attacks up to mid-1943 had not yet involved concerted attempts to penetrate deep into German airspace, they had brought about a significant strengthening of the German home-defence force, from about 450 to 1,100 day fighters. Despite Anglo-American efforts to bomb aircraft factories, German fighter production increased through 1943 right up to September 1944.

HEAVY LOSSES

The first big tests of the US commanders' belief that their bombers could fight their way to their targets unescorted came in August 1943. On the 1st the Mediterranean force lost very heavily in a raid on the oilfields at Ploesti in Romania. On 17 August some 376 US bombers attacked the Messerschmitt factory at Regensburg and the ball-bearing manufacturing plant at Schweinfurt; 60 bombers were lost and Schweinfurt in particular was little damaged.

Even though part of the bomber escort was made up of P-47 Thunderbolts fitted with longer-range fuel tanks, these could reach only just inside Germany; most of the losses were on the long unescorted leg of the mission between there and the target and back again.

Confirmation of the desperate need for longer-range escort fighters came in October. A series of raids, including one on Schweinfurt on the 14th, cost

Eighth AF about half its operational strength. The American commanders abandoned deep-penetration attacks for the moment. The Luftwaffe had won the first round of the battle.

Right: General Ira Eaker, seen in 1942. Eaker commanded Eighth Air Force during its unsuccessful operations in 1943.

Clearing the Ukraine

Between mid-summer 1943 and late spring 1944 a series of crushing Soviet attacks drove the Germans out of the Ukraine, pushing them back into pre-war Poland and Romania. In the north the 900-day siege of Leningrad was also lifted.

From the conclusion of the Kursk offensive to the end of the war a little less than two years later, the Red Army would advance relentlessly and almost continuously for victory.

In the first phase of the battles the Soviets pushed forward all along the southern two-thirds of the front, to reach and cross the Dniepr River and recover such major cities as Smolensk, Kiev and Dnepropetrovsk. In the second phase, in the winter and early spring of 1944, there

Above: German soldiers in the cold and snow of an Eastern Front winter, March 1944.

were attacks in the north and south. In the north the bitter siege of Leningrad was finally broken; in the south the rest of the Ukraine was recaptured and the first steps were taken toward the conquest of southeastern Europe.

TO THE DNIEPR

The process began with Soviet attacks on the north of the Kursk salient on 12 July and was extended by a further offensive on the south flank of the salient on 3 August. Although the Germans defended very skilfully against these advances, they had to give up Orel to the northern drive in early August and Kharkov to the southern attack on the 23rd.

By the end of August Soviet forces were advancing everywhere south of Moscow – but especially successfully in a broad area west of Kursk and in another sector in the far south toward Stalino (Donetsk).

Aware of the possible Italian surrender (which became a reality on 8 September), Hitler had already begun to reinforce his troops in Italy. Allied landings on mainland Italy in early September made this still more urgent. He therefore gave permission for the German troops in the eastern Ukraine to retreat

SOVIET VICTORIES, 1943–4
The Red Army's advances cleared the Germans from most of the territory of the pre-war USSR.

Map

0   100   200   300 mi
0   200   400 km

Gulf of Riga

Riga

MOSCOW

U S S R

Smolensk

Minsk   Orel

Bialystok   Kursk

Mozyr

Brest   Sarny   Belgorod

Kiev   Kharkov

Lubny   Izyum

Lvov   Vinnitsa   Voroshilovgrad

Rostov

Sea of Azov

Odessa   Perekop

Novorossiysk

Sevastopol   Yalta

Black Sea

Legend:
- ➤ Soviet attacks
- ➤ German attacks
- —— Front line 4 July 1943
- --- Front line 30 Sept 1943
- -·-· Front line 23 Dec 1943
- -··-·· Front line 24 Jan 1944
- ······ Front line mid-Apr 1944

SIEGE OF LENINGRAD

In terms of its effect on the outcome of the war, the siege of Leningrad (St Petersburg) was a sideshow at most. However, with probably more than a million civilians dead, most by starvation, disease and cold, it was a human tragedy on a vast scale.

By early September 1941 the Germans' first advances had cut Leningrad off from the rest of the USSR, and Hitler decided to obliterate the city by bombing, shelling and starvation. The Soviet authorities had delayed evacuating the civilian population of 2.5 million: about a third were evacuated in 1942; a third remained in the city, fighting or working in the factories; and a third died in the first dreadful winter.

For more than a year, despite attacks and counterattacks by both sides, a trickle of supplies (but only that) reached the city across Lake Ladoga. The supplies travelled by boat in summer and by truck over the ice in winter, but all the time under German shelling and air attack. New Soviet attacks in January 1943 opened up a narrow land route into the city, easing the worst privations, but got no further. Finally, in January 1944, a new offensive forced a general German retreat. Stalin declared the city liberated on the 27th.

to the Dniepr. As they did so they converged on the various major towns with bridges over the river. The Soviets advanced into the gaps between these and had improvised crossings themselves by the end of the month north of Kiev and west of Dnepropetrovsk. Kiev itself was taken in early November.

ON TO THE BORDERS

By December, despite the able defensive leadership of Field Marshals Erich von Manstein and Ewald von Kleist, the German front included a number of vulnerable salients, held on Hitler's orders. In attacks

Above: Red Army soldiers receive a warm welcome from local people after the recapture of Kiev.

beginning on 24 December and extending through March 1944, these were eliminated at the start of new advances. Both field marshals joined the growing list of able German generals dismissed for making withdrawals and arguing too often with their erratic *Führer*.

When this phase of fighting ended in mid-April, the front line ran from the Pripet Marshes via the eastern foothills of the Carpathian Mountains to the Black Sea coast west of Odessa.

Left: German troops on the retreat with a horse-drawn 5cm (1.97in) PaK 38 anti-tank gun in the Ukraine in the mud of the spring thaw, 1944.

The Soviet Invasion of Germany Fighting in the German town of Küstrin in early 1945.

Totalitarian Rule, Germany and the USSR Inmates of the Sachsenhausen concentration camp.

Resistance Female fighters of the French resistance greet the liberation of Marseille in 1944.

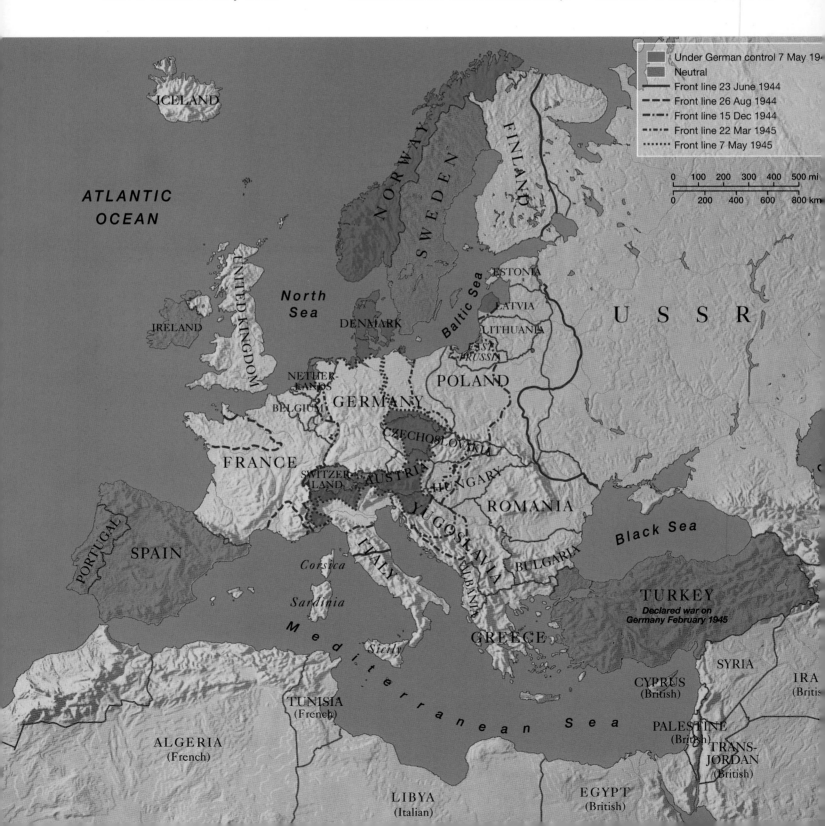

ICELAND

ATLANTIC
OCEAN

NORWAY

SWEDEN

FINLAND

North
Sea

Baltic Sea

ESTONIA

LATVIA

LITHUANIA

IRELAND

UNITED KINGDOM

DENMARK

E. SS.
PRUSSIA

USSR

NETHER-
LANDS

POLAND

BELGIUM

GERMANY

FRANCE

SWITZER-
LAND

CZECHOSLOVAKIA

AUSTRIA

HUNGARY

ROMANIA

PORTUGAL

SPAIN

Corsica

ITALY

YUGOSLAVIA

ALBANIA

BULGARIA

Black Sea

Sardinia

TURKEY

*Declared war on
Germany February 1945*

GREECE

Sicily

Mediterranean Sea

SYRIA

CYPRUS
(British)

IRA
(Britis

TUNISIA
(French)

PALESTINE
(British)

ALGERIA
(French)

TRANS-
JORDAN
(British)

LIBYA
(Italian)

EGYPT
(British)

Under German control 7 May 19
Neutral
Front line 23 June 1944
Front line 26 Aug 1944
Front line 15 Dec 1944
Front line 22 Mar 1945
Front line 7 May 1945

0   100   200   300   400   500 mi
0   200   400   600   800 km

VICTORY OVER GERMANY

By early 1944 Hitler's Kriegsmarine had been reduced virtually to impotence in the Battle of the Atlantic and that spring the Luftwaffe was decisively defeated in a titanic series of air battles over Germany. Yet, at the start of June, German soldiers stood everywhere on foreign soil and even still maintained a toehold inside the pre-war USSR. By the early autumn the Western Allies had liberated France, Hitler's armies in the east had suffered the devastating defeat known as the destruction of Army Group Centre, and among his erstwhile allies Romania had changed sides and Finland made peace.

Hitler himself, weakened and shaken by his injuries in the Bomb Plot assassination attempt, was increasingly out of touch with reality, while the German economy and its industries were heading into their final collapse. But, despite all that, the German Army remained a formidable and resourceful organization, capable of desperate defence and last-ditch counter-attacks. The true nature of the Nazi regime was finally made plain to all with the liberation of the concentration camps in the spring of 1945, but the European war would not end until almost all of Germany was in Allied hands and Hitler was dead in the ruins of Berlin, capital city of his vaunted "thousand-year *Reich*".

Fighters, 1943–5 A Supermarine Spitfire Mark 14 fighter in flight, the final major production version.

The Battle for Normandy US Army artillerymen in action on the Cotentin Peninsula.

The Fall of Berlin Soviet troops raise their flag over the Reichstag building at the centre of the city.

D-Day

Operation Overlord had been the centrepiece of Anglo-American plans since 1942 and was the largest combined land–sea–air operation in history. The Germans ultimately would have no answer to the Allied firepower and strength.

By the end of 6 June 1944 the Allies had landed some 150,000 men in Normandy. All five landing beaches were secure and everywhere the troops were pushing inland, though not as far as had been hoped and planned. The first day of Operation Overlord had been at least a qualified success.

THE PLANS

Although the Allies had a crushing superiority in the air and at sea, the actual landing forces were not overwhelmingly strong because of limited numbers of landing craft and paratroop aircraft. Several strategies were used to offset this. Months of intensive air attacks had been

Right: German troops building beach defences before D-Day run for cover from an Allied aircraft.

KEY FACTS

PLACE: Lower Normandy, France

DATE: 6 June 1944

OUTCOME: Allied air and seaborne landings succeeded despite strong German resistance.

---

carried out and would continue against roads, rail lines and bridges all across France, with the aim of making it difficult for the Germans to move reinforcements to Normandy.

At the same time an elaborate deception plan had been set up to convince the Germans that the Allies planned to land farther east in the Pas de Calais region. This continued after the landings to suggest that Normandy was a feint and the real Pas de Calais operation was yet to come. Both phases were extremely successful.

The Allied Supreme Commander, General Dwight D. Eisenhower, led over 3 million men with 13,000 aircraft, 2,500 landing craft, 1,200 warships and a range of new equipment. This included the obstacle-crossing and bunker-busting tanks of the British 79th Armoured Division, used only on the Anglo-Canadian beaches, as well as amphibious tanks used by all attack formations. Follow-up forces would benefit from the Mulberry Harbours and have their fuel needs supplied by PLUTO (Pipe Line Under The Ocean).

Although the Germans were well aware that there would be an invasion, they had no

D-DAY PLANS

The Allied attack forces came from bases across the British Isles. German forces were inevitably spread out along the French coast.

Assault forces
Follow-up units
Airborne forces
Assault
Follow-up formations
German units
German infantry divisions
Panzer divisions

Above: A British commando unit on Sword Beach waits for the order to advance inland.

Above: US Army troops landing on the bitterly contested Omaha Beach on the morning of D-Day.

accurate intelligence of its location or strength. Field Marshal Erwin Rommel now commanded the German forces in northern France. He believed that his only chance was to defeat the invasion before it got properly ashore. He wanted to spread his reserves along the coast so that they could immediately attack any landing forces, because he knew the Allied air forces would make it very difficult to redeploy more distant units.

His superior, Commander-in-Chief West Field Marshal Gerd von Rundstedt, wanted a strong central reserve that would only be sent into the attack once it was clear where the main Allied landings were taking place. The Germans ended up with a compromise: some reserves were near the Normandy coast, but they were not allowed to be deployed without permission from Hitler.

THE LANDINGS

There were five landing areas – Utah, Omaha, Gold, Juno and Sword, from west to east. The first two involved units of US First Army and the last three

British and Canadians of British Second Army. Two US airborne divisions landed by parachute and glider inland from Utah and one British airborne division on the east flank of Sword.

The airborne divisions took most of their objectives and succeeded in disrupting possible enemy counter-attacks. German resistance was fiercest, and Allied casualties heaviest, on Omaha Beach. For a time it looked as if the landing there might fail, but by the end of the day the beach had been cleared. Utah was the easiest of all – with the other three beaches somewhere in between.

Above: One of the vast armament dumps in the UK created by the Allies in preparation for D-Day.

It was important for the Allied troops to grab as much territory as possible at the outset, even if only to make room for the vast follow-up forces. However, the inland advance later in the day came up well short of the D-Day objectives of Caen and Bayeux. Much hard fighting to expand the beachheads clearly lay ahead.

MULBERRY HARBOURS

Since the speed with which supplies and reinforcements could be landed was crucial, and capturing a port would be difficult, the Allied planners decided to solve the problem by taking their own "Mulberry Harbours" with them. Huge breakwaters, causeways and piers were built in Britain, floated across the Channel and then sunk in place off Normandy in the first couple of weeks after D-Day. Two Mulberries were built. One was wrecked in a storm on 19 June, but the other remained in use until late 1944.

The Battle for Normandy

It took two months of bitter combat before the Allied forces were able to break out of their Normandy landing areas. The Allies had overwhelming resources and dominated the air, but German battlefield skill made them fight all the way.

The success or failure of Operation Overlord was not likely to be decided on 6 June 1944. The Allies made vast and elaborate preparations to ensure that D-Day would go well, but in the light of these it was overwhelmingly likely to do so. What mattered, in the days and weeks to come, was building up the Allied force and the area under its control faster than the Germans could assemble their reserves to confine it.

MONTGOMERY'S PLAN

All the Allied ground forces, British, American and Canadian, were under the command of General Montgomery's 21st Army Group. Probably more than any other general on the Allied side, he realized that if the Normandy invasion were to succeed, the Allies had to have a clear plan for the advance inland

Above: An American field artillery unit in action near the Normandy town of Carentan during the fighting in July 1944.

from the beaches. Montgomery developed such a plan and stuck to it so successfully that throughout the battle the Germans largely danced to his tune. His failure was that he never admitted when parts of the plan went astray. Thus, his relationship with other top Allied leaders was poor and his presentation of events to the press was unconvincing.

Montgomery's plan was for British and Canadian attacks on the Allied left to draw in the German reserves, while allowing the American units on the right to advance more rapidly.

Left: British troops on the watch for German snipers amid the rubble of Caen in late July.

Right: American infantrymen move cautiously past a burning Panther tank in a Normandy village.

This, in essence, is exactly what happened. However, it certainly did not all go "according to plan", though Montgomery claimed that it did.

The city and communications centre of Caen on the left (eastern) flank was meant to be captured on D-Day itself, but the advance from the beaches only got about halfway there. Caen did not fall completely until the third week of July, after several full-scale attacks by British Second Army, notably Operation Epsom at the end of June and Goodwood in July.

On the right flank the first task was to link the Utah and Omaha landings with the other beaches, which was achieved on 10 June. Next was an advance west across the Cotentin Peninsula and then north to capture Cherbourg, which was taken on 27 June. The port facilities, however, had been comprehensively wrecked by the Germans before their surrender. It would take many weeks to rebuild the port to full capacity, though it would land some cargoes during July.

GERMAN RESISTANCE

All the Allied forces were discovering just how tough the German armed forces were to beat, whether the best Army units like the Panzer Lehr Division or the teenage SS fanatics of the Hitler Youth Division. At all junior and middle-rank levels the standard of German leadership was higher overall, and the German troops fought in the knowledge that their tanks in particular were vastly better than anything the Allies had. However, the Allied generals were playing ever more solidly to their armies' strengths, in particular deploying a weight of artillery and air firepower to which the Germans could have no answer.

Through June into July US First Army was thus slowly and steadily gaining ground, while British Second Army was seemingly bogged down at Caen. Montgomery would have been delighted to have captured Caen sooner and pushed inland from there, but even without that his plan was working. Almost all the German Panzer divisions, the backbone of their force, were fighting on the British sector of the front. This prepared the ground for the decisive Allied breakout against the weaker part of the German line to the west of St-Lô in First Army's Operation Cobra from 25 July.

Below: US troops fighting near Périers during the advance across the Cotentin Peninsula.

Resistance

*Many people in occupied Europe judged that the defeat of Nazi Germany was a
cause worth risking their lives for. Their bravery and sacrifice certainly
played a large part in ensuring the ultimate Allied victory.*

By its nature much resistance was a secret activity with few records kept. Many heroic acts no doubt also went unseen, so it is now impossible to quantify the effects of resistance in any meaningful way.

Resistance was certainly dangerous. Suspected resisters were routinely tortured and, if not executed, sent to concentration camps. Vicious mass reprisals against their communities were common. Unsurprisingly, therefore, more people took an active part in resistance as Germany's defeat became more certain, and those most active at the end were not necessarily those who had the best record throughout.

Resistance took many forms and might not even have had any long-term effect on the war.

Above: Resistance fighters of the Polish Home Army in action during the Warsaw Rising of 1944.

Norwegian history teachers, for example, refused to teach the Nazi-approved syllabus and stood firm to win their point, despite some being deported to concentration camps. Other more significant forms of quiet heroism came from those who hid Jews from the SS, many thousands in Poland and the Netherlands alone.

Some non-violent methods had clear military results. French railway workers deliberately doing their jobs slowly and incompetently may have done more to hinder the movement of German troops and supplies in France in 1944 than the Allied bombers or the active sabotage efforts of their resistance comrades. Similarly, up to 2,000 Anglo-American aircrew who had been shot down were helped to escape from German-occupied territory, an important increment to Allied strength.

ALLIED ASSISTANCE

The Western Allies had various organizations that supported resistance. The USA's Office of Strategic Services (OSS) was involved both in intelligence-gathering (clearly an important function of resistance generally) and the support of military resistance. Britain split these functions between the secret service, MI6, and the wartime Special Operations Executive (SOE). Britain's MI9 and the American MIS-X helped escapees and those who assisted

Left: Resisters in newly liberated Marseille show off their weapons. Resistance was one area in which female combatants played a full part.

them. SOE and OSS trained many operatives for covert service in the occupied countries and had extensive technical sections designing and making special weapons, forging identity documents and carrying out many similar tasks.

HORROR IN YUGOSLAVIA

Resistance fighting was most intense of all in Yugoslavia. At the end of the war the Partisan movement, led by Josip Broz Tito and by then backed by both the Soviets and the West, effectively liberated the country from the Germans after four years of particularly bloody struggle. The Partisans were the victors after what was really a civil war between them, the Četniks (mainly Serbian nationalists) and the Ustašas (mostly Croatian fascists). Each fought the others and with and against the occupying Germans and Italians at different times. Most of the 1 million plus Yugoslavs who died during the war were killed by other Yugoslavs.

The situation in Western Europe was never as extreme, as the example of France shows. There was certainly tension and distrust between communist and non-communist resistance groups, but almost the whole resistance movement agreed in 1943 to work together under the command of the Free French leaders in exile. In 1944 there were extensive and successful plans to co-ordinate resistance

Right: Josip Broz Tito (nearest camera), leader of the Yugoslav Partisan movement, meeting "Draža" Mihailović (dark hair in front row) of the rival Četnik group, which initially received most Allied support.

operations with the Normandy invasion. Many resisters were young men who had taken to the hills and forests to avoid compulsory work service in Germany. These Maquis groups played a notably important part in assisting the Allied invasion

Above: General Charles de Gaulle, leader of the Free French, making a broadcast to his countrymen.

of southern France. Perhaps 100,000 French people died in resistance activities or in German reprisals against them.

Collaboration

Collaborators had many motives. Some genuinely supported Nazi ideas; some were merely trying to survive as best they could in impossible circumstances; and some thought of themselves as patriots honestly trying to serve their countries.

Who were collaborators? Government ministers in occupied countries who decided in the early-war period to work with the Germans could be regarded as collaborators – or were they just being realistic in making the best arrangements they could with the country that had effectively won the war? Industrialists might run factories making goods for the Germans and money for themselves, but they were also keeping their workers in decent jobs and preventing them being deported as slave labour to Germany. A village mayor or a policeman had no choice but to obey some German orders, but when did he go beyond that into enthusiastic help? And, at the simplest level of all, was a

Above: A Waffen-SS poster seeks Norwegian recruits to fight against communism. Norwegians and Danes were eagerly enlisted by the SS.

woman in a relationship with a German soldier a shameful traitor or in fact doing something all too human with a young man scared and far from his home? It was not always easy to decide.

Almost every country had native fascists and anti-semites who worked willingly with the Nazis, genuinely believing that they were acting patriotically. For example, Anton Mussert's party in the Netherlands had 50,000 members. But he, and his like elsewhere, were given no real power by the Germans.

Poland was probably the country that saw the least collaboration with the Germans, but even there another kind of collaboration was seen. Many pro-communist Poles helped the Soviets consolidate their control from 1944, and would have been seen as collaborators by most of their compatriots.

JOINING THE SS

Putting on a German uniform and fighting for the Germans was certainly collaboration in most people's eyes. In fact many people born outside Germany enlisted in the Nazi Party's armed elite, the Waffen-SS. They included both ethnic Germans recruited from abroad – *Volksdeutsche* (as the Nazis

Left: Women who had relationships with Germans being forced to parade through the streets of Paris with shaved heads and in their underclothes after the liberation.

Right: Dutch Nazi leader Anton Mussert (in black) meeting SS chief Heinrich Himmler.

called them) – and foreigners from "Germanic" countries like Norway or Denmark. Later in the war the net was cast wider; Ukrainians, Croatian Muslims, Latvians, Estonians and others were all accepted. Eventually, over half of Waffen-SS soldiers were not native Germans.

Substantial numbers of Soviet citizens ended up working for, and sometimes fighting alongside, the German Army. By 1942 many of Germany's units included significant numbers of auxiliaries – *Hilfswillige* (or "Hiwis"). Many of these were former prisoners of war who had made this choice to escape the privations and likely death of captivity. At first they worked mainly in non-combatant support roles, as drivers, cooks and the like, but later they became fighting troops. In Normandy in 1944 German Army regiments regularly included an *Ostbataillon* (or "East Battalion") of such men and some fought effectively.

RUSSIAN NATIONALISTS

Other units that were formed by the Germans attempted to use anti-Soviet feeling and even appeal to Russian nationalism. These included various units of non-Slav Soviet citizens – Cossacks, Armenians, Georgians and others – who often fought in anti-partisan operations. Russians as such were also involved. A Russian National

Right: Many of the recruits for the Waffen-SS Handschar Division were Bosnian and Croatian Muslims.

Army of Liberation was formed in the Bryansk region. Better known as the Kaminsky Brigade, it gained a brutal reputation, notably during the Warsaw Rising of 1944.

A senior Red Army officer, General Andrei Vlasov, was captured in 1942 and agreed to raise a substantial anti-Stalinist Russian force. Top-level German support was half-hearted and only two divisions were formed,

but not used. In the last days of the war one of these turned against the Germans and fought alongside the Czech resistance during the battle for Prague.

The post-war fate of identified collaborators was often harsh. Millions of Soviet citizens were turned over to the Soviet authorities by the Western Allies. Most ended up in the GULag at best; Vlasov and his officers were executed.

Crushing Soviet Victories, 1944

The summer battles of 1944 began with what Soviet historians call the "destruction of Army Group Centre", and by the end of the year Romania and Bulgaria were fighting alongside the Soviets with the front line well into Poland and Hungary.

Misled by the Soviet advance into Romania in the spring of 1944, Hitler and his generals expected the Soviets to continue to concentrate on the southern part of the front for their next big attacks. Accordingly they transferred most of the tanks and many other heavy weapons from German Army Group Centre in Belorussia, just at the time when the Soviets were concentrating over 2 million troops and vast resources to attack it.

ADVANCE IN BELORUSSIA

The attacks began on 23 June and, partly because of the unimaginative command of Field Marshal Ernst Busch (who was quickly replaced), soon smashed the German front. Three German armies – Third Panzer, Fourth and Ninth – each lost the majority of their

Above: A horse-drawn Soviet 45mm (1.77in) anti-tank unit advancing into Poland in 1944.

strength, around 400,000 men in all. Minsk, the offensive's initial target, was captured on 11 July.

To the north Soviet attacks beginning on 4 July cleared the Germans out of much of Latvia and Lithuania by the end of August. By November virtually all the Baltic States were in Soviet hands, except for the

Courland Peninsula, where some 20 German divisions would hold out until the end of the war. Finland, allied with Germany since 1941, had also been attacked in June; and the Finns then agreed an armistice with the Soviets in September.

During July the Soviet Belorussian fronts continued their advances at pace and were joined by new attacks by the Ukrainian fronts to the south. Brest-Litovsk and Lvov were both taken late in the month. By 15 August Soviet troops were on the east bank of the Vistula River opposite Warsaw.

WARSAW UPRISING

Resistance fighters of the Polish Home Army had already been helping the Soviet advance and on 1 August they began an all-out uprising in Warsaw. They fought on until early October, by which time over 200,000 Poles had been killed.

The Soviets made no attempt to help them, claiming (not entirely implausibly) that they needed to resupply their front-line forces after the recent advances before they tried to cross the Vistula. However, it also suited Stalin's grim purpose to have the Germans kill off anti-communist Polish patriots for him. Similarly, when Slovaks rose against the Germans in late

Left: Red Army infantry moving up to the front for the Soviet attack on Lvov in July 1944.

Above: Soviet infantry assault pass a burning Panther tank, eastern Poland, summer 1944.

August, the Soviets did little to help. This rising was also largely put down by late October.

INTO THE BALKANS

With its northern forces halting on the Vistula, the Red Army began new attacks in the far south on 20 August. Within days much of German Sixth Army was destroyed near Kishinev. King Michael of Romania mounted a coup on 23 August and his new government brought the country (and its large army) into the war on the Soviet side.

As the German forces continued their fighting retreat through Romania and into Hungary, Bulgaria was next to fall. The last in a sequence of government changes brought a partly communist group to power on 9 September, the day after Soviet troops had crossed into Bulgaria from Romania. The Bulgarians, too, would now join the Allied forces on the Eastern Front, while some Soviet troops remained in their country to ensure communist control.

With these threatening advances to their rear, German troops began pulling out of Greece and Yugoslavia. Yugoslav Partisans liberated Belgrade on 19 October and by the end of the year controlled roughly half of their country. British troops from Italy arrived in Greece to take over there in October too.

By December the Germans had again managed to build a defensive front. The principal fighting was in Hungary, where Budapest was surrounded on 26 December and would endure a bitter siege until mid-February.

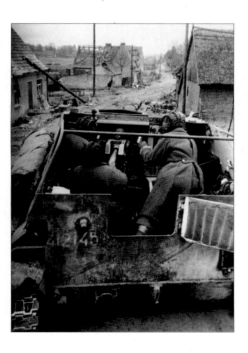

GEORGI ZHUKOV

Marshal Zhukov (1896–1974) was the leading Soviet soldier of the war. His first big achievement was the decisive defeat of the Japanese at Khalkhin Gol in 1939. In 1941–2 he was repeatedly switched between staff jobs and front commands by Stalin. He was credited with masterminding the defence of Leningrad, Moscow and Stalingrad, although in each case the timing of his arrival was fortuitous. Zhukov then directed various of the Red Army advances up to and including the capture of Berlin in 1945. As a commander he was ruthless and thorough, one of many such leading generals who made the shambolic Red Army of 1941 into the world's most feared fighting force by 1945.

Above: Marshal Zhukov during the advance to Berlin in 1945.

Left: An SU-76 assault gun in action in a village in south-eastern Europe during the Soviet advance in the late summer of 1944.

Totalitarian Rule: Germany and the USSR

For all that the two countries were the bitterest enemies, there were many close comparisons in the methods of government in Nazi Germany and the USSR, starting with the cruel and murderous nature of the regimes.

It is hardly surprising that there were a great many similarities between Nazi Germany and the Communist USSR in the WWII period. Both countries were dominated by a single political party whose organs and whose secret police featured in every corner of national life. And at their head was a single ruler with the power of life and death and absolute control over every aspect of state policy.

POLICE AND SECURITY

Both countries' regimes had a unified apparatus for security, policing and public discipline matters. In Germany the Reich Main Security Office (RSHA), a major division of Heinrich

Below: One of the 1944 Bomb Plotters faces the ranting Nazi judge Roland Freisler at his show trial before his inevitable execution.

Above: Lavrenti Beria controlled the USSR's security apparatus from 1938–53, murdering at Stalin's command and for his own pleasure.

Himmler's SS, was the controlling body. Its main chiefs were first Reinhard Heydrich and later Ernst Kaltenbrunner; its subordinate departments included the SS security service and the Gestapo secret police. The RSHA was surprisingly small, only some 50,000 people in all in 1944, but it also maintained an extensive network of informers all too ready to denounce "defeatists" or "asocials".

In the USSR the organization varied at different times in the war but included both the NKVD and NKGB. However, both came under the control of Lavrenti Beria, the Commissar for State Security. Unlike the rather squeamish Himmler, who disliked personal involvement

in the atrocities he ordered, Beria was himself a vicious and enthusiastic torturer and killer.

The principal instruments of coercion in both countries were the prison camps. No one knows how many unfortunates suffered in the Soviet camps, the GULag, but it is clear that to be sent to the camps was virtually a death sentence. Estimates suggest that during the war 1 million prisoners a year died of overwork, starvation and every other kind of cruelty. The process of selection was haphazard; many prisoners had done nothing to offend the regime.

Most of those in Germany's concentration camps were in some way obnoxious to the Nazis: habitual criminals, left-wingers and many more. At first prisoners were at least meant to be kept alive to work (the death camps where Jews were sent had a different mission). Camp prisoners slaved in vile conditions in quarries, mines and factories – many run as highly profitable businesses by the SS. Half a million is a common estimate of the number who died in the concentration camps.

Discipline in the armed forces was also stunningly harsh. The German Army executed at least 10,000 of its men (and probably many more) for military crimes like cowardice and desertion. (The US Army executed one.) The Red Army had numerous punishment units to which several hundred thousand men were sent for astonishingly trivial reasons. These units were used on repeated near-suicidal missions, which few of their soldiers survived.

THE HOME FRONTS

Generally speaking civilian life was relatively comfortable for Germans until 1943 at least. Rations were reasonable; consumer goods were available; women were not required to do war work; and many prosperous families even had servants.

None of this was true in the USSR. Only workers in important industries got rations much above starvation levels. Millions of people were moved to the new industrial and mining areas out of the Germans' reach. Employees in the new factories built in 1941–2 often started work before the roof was even on

and slept among the machines because they had no houses. Remarkably they did so very willingly on the whole, a level of commitment that was central to the USSR's victory in what its leaders taught the people to call the Great Patriotic War.

Indeed despite all the cruelties of the ruling regimes, the German and Soviet peoples fought hard for their countries throughout the war.

Right: A German poster appealing for donations of old clothes and woollens for the war effort.

Below: Prisoners at the Nazi Sachsenhausen concentration camp in 1938. About 100,000 died there.

ASSASSINATING HITLER

There were several attempts to assassinate Hitler. The most nearly successful was on 20 July 1944, when he was injured by a bomb placed in his conference room. The group of officers responsible planned a military coup, but this fell apart when it became clear Hitler had survived. About 5,000 people were executed in the aftermath. Hitler became even more mentally unstable than before and trusted his generals even less.

The Defeat of the Luftwaffe

American air victories over Germany in early 1944 set both the British and American bomber forces free to smash Germany's war effort. Heavily outnumbered and practically out of fuel, the Luftwaffe could do little to resist.

Two vital command decisions ensured the crushing defeat of the Luftwaffe in early 1944. Although the leaders of the American bomber force had not fully appreciated the importance of fighter escorts for their attacks, in late October 1943 General "Hap" Arnold, Chief of Staff of the USAAF, ordered that all P-51 Mustang production for the next three months was to go to Eighth AF for bomber support. The second decision came in January 1944 when General James Doolittle, new commander of Eighth AF, ordered his fighters not to be tied to the close-escort mission but to seek out and destroy their German counterparts. Together these set the scene for a series of massive air battles in which the USAAF would win air superiority over Germany.

Early 1944 saw RAF Bomber Command continuing to lose heavily in the Battle of Berlin. This culminated in a disastrous attack on Nuremberg on the night of 30–31 March, in which 96 out of 795 bombers were lost. Although Air Marshal Harris bitterly opposed the decision and made as many "area bombing" attacks on German targets as he could get away with, it was fortunate for his men that they were mainly sent against targets in France, over the next several months, in support of the coming D-Day landings.

"BIG WEEK"

The first real chance for the American forces to put the new policy into effect came in mid-February, in a series of attacks on the German aircraft industry known as "Big Week". Contrary to what the Allies believed at the time, these barely dented German aircraft production, which continued to increase until September 1944 because of improved organization. Nor was there a clear-cut victory for either side in the air – the American forces lost some 250 bombers in return for 355

Left: A reconnaissance photo of bomb craters around the Dortmund–Ems Canal. Once used to transport U-boat parts, the canal was emptied by RAF attacks in late 1944.

Above: A camera-gun picture from a British fighter shooting down an Fw 190 trying to attack a Lancaster bomber over Germany in late 1944.

German fighters downed. However, over 100 irreplaceable German pilots were killed. Fighter-pilot training and experience levels on the American side were on the increase; other than for a diminishing band of top aces, the reverse was now true for the Germans.

The process continued relentlessly, notably with missions to Berlin itself in March. Even though the US heavy bombers, like RAF Bomber Command, came under General Eisenhower's control on 1 April in preparation for D-Day, they continued to make some telling attacks on targets in Germany and Central Europe.

OIL ATTACKS

From May both the USAAF and RAF Bomber Command made an increasing number of strikes on Germany's synthetic oil production sites. Although Harris had been right to deride previous attempts to pick off key German target systems as ineffective "panaceas", this proved to be something different. By September 1944 German aviation fuel production was around 7 per cent of the already inadequate level achieved in May.

This hampered operations and made training of the new pilots now in urgent demand virtually impossible. Those who did leave the training system were increasingly easy meat for the better prepared Allied fighters.

In August, in perhaps the clearest token of how things had changed, RAF Bomber Command returned to daylight operations over Germany. From then until attacks were wound down in the final weeks of the war, both British and American heavy bombers ranged almost at will over Germany, flattening cities and devastating industries with a weight of destructive power and levels of accuracy out of all proportion to anything ever before achieved.

Below: A damaged B-17 Flying Fortress drops its bombs on Berlin during a raid in August 1944.

DRESDEN

Since the war, and to some degree during it, some people have questioned the morality of heavy-bomber attacks on enemy populations and have doubted whether they were an efficient use of resources. The bombing by the RAF of the city of Dresden on 13–14 February 1945 has been particularly controversial. There were no military targets of importance in the city and it was packed with refugees, yet it was smashed by over 700 bombers and as many as 70,000 or perhaps more people were killed.

Above: Bodies litter the streets of Dresden after the attacks.

From Normandy to the Rhine

At the end of July 1944 the continued Allied pressure in Normandy finally cracked the German front. Within a month the Allied troops had liberated most of France and Belgium but hopes of winning the war in 1944 would soon be abandoned.

On 25 July US First Army was able to begin Operation Cobra to break out from the Normandy bridgehead. Over the next few days the attack made good progress south past Avranches. By 1 August the German front in the area had crumbled away and a new Allied formation, US Third Army led by General George Patton, burst out into the open. Part of Third Army cleared Brittany to the west, eventually taking the ports of St-Malo and Brest, but other units headed south-east for Le Mans and the interior of France.

Hitler now intervened. Although all the other Allied forces were also pushing foward and his generals were sensibly beginning to think about a retreat, he ordered an attack through Mortain to Avranches to cut off the Third Army advance where it began. This attack was fought to a standstill on 7–8 August and by then the whole German force in Normandy was in deep trouble.

THE FALAISE POCKET

Around 20 divisions were caught in a pocket between British and Canadians in the north and Americans in the south. They had no option but to retreat frantically to the east past Falaise, while trying to fend off Allied attacks all the way. Although many of the German troops in the so-called Falaise Pocket did manage to escape before its neck was closed, they no longer formed effective military formations. And, to complete the Allied victory in Normandy, Allied troops were already across the River Seine west of Paris.

There was yet more bad news for the Germans. On 15 August French and American troops landed on the Mediterranean coast between Cannes and Toulon. The German forces in southern France were too weak to provide real opposition and were also being seriously harassed by French resistance fighters. By the end of August the invasion force was advancing steadily up the Rhône Valley

LIBERATION OF FRANCE
After a long and bitter struggle in Normandy, Allied forces liberated the rest of France in only a few weeks.

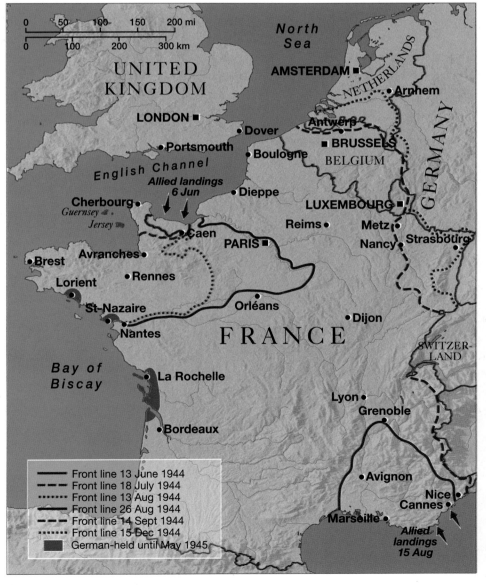

Legend:
- Front line 13 June 1944
- Front line 18 July 1944
- Front line 13 Aug 1944
- Front line 26 Aug 1944
- Front line 14 Sept 1944
- Front line 15 Dec 1944
- German-held until May 1945

Above: Allied Sherman tanks crossing the Nijmegen Bridge on their way to Arnhem.

Above: Many German troops and vehicles were hit by Allied air attacks in the Falaise Pocket.

and would link up with troops advancing from Normandy on 12 September.

After the slow slog through Normandy the campaign was transformed. Paris was liberated on 25 August. By the end of the month most of France was free and most of Belgium followed in the next few days. By now, the Allied forces were out-running their supply resources and the top generals were arguing over what to do next. The port of Antwerp, which had the capacity to land all the supplies the armies were likely to need, had fallen on 4 September, but its estuary was still in German hands. The best plan would probably have been to have immediately mounted a campaign to clear the estuary and solve the supply problems, but this was not done until October and the first cargoes were not landed until late November.

A BRIDGE TOO FAR

Instead Montgomery persuaded Eisenhower, the Supreme Commander, that the best plan was to cross the series of river barriers blocking the route into Germany in a joint airborne and ground-forces attack. Operation Market Garden seized several major bridges but the last, over the Rhine at Arnhem, could not be taken. The Allied advance ground to a halt all along the front by the end of September.

While the British and Canadian forces were finally clearing the Scheldt estuary, the American armies were fighting hard for small gains around Aachen and in the Saar and Moselle regions to the south. It was an autumn and early winter of bitter disappointment after the high hopes of only weeks before. And the Germans were recovering fast from their Normandy disaster and assembling reserves for a new attack.

GENERAL GEORGE PATTON

Patton (1885–1945) was probably the most able American general of the war, though his talents were marred by showmanship and a love of publicity. He successfully commanded US troops in North Africa and Sicily but was then sidelined for a time after striking two hospitalized soldiers he wrongly accused of malingering. He commanded US Third Army in 1944–5, leading it particularly brilliantly during the advance in August 1944 and in the Battle of the Bulge in December.

Right: General Patton, photographed shortly before the Sicilian campaign during which he quarrelled fiercely with General Montgomery.

Battle of the Bulge

Hitler aimed to repeat the triumph of 1940 in an attack through the Ardennes region to cut the Allied armies in two. Instead Germany's last reserves were defeated in a series of desperate winter battles.

By the late autumn of 1944 the German Army had recovered some of its strength after the disasters of both the summer in Normandy and the Eastern Front. However, the American armies were pushing forward slowly in eastern France and Belgium, while the British had finally succeeded in clearing the Scheldt estuary, so that the great port facilities of Antwerp could at long last begin to alleviate the Allied supply problems.

Hitler decided to use the assembling German reserve force in the west, where he was convinced a major success would bring quarrels between

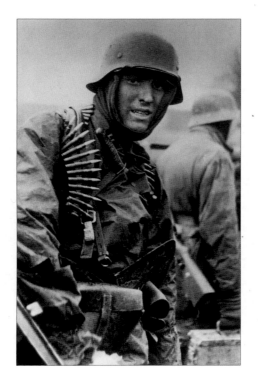

Below: Draped with machine-gun ammunition and much other equipment, an SS trooper prepares to attack during the Ardennes battle.

Above: An M36 tank destroyer in the Ardennes. The M36's 90mm (3.54in) gun was the best US anti-tank weapon in 1944–5.

Britain and the USA, persuade them to make peace and perhaps even join him in fighting the Soviets. The plan was to advance through the Ardennes region, just as in May 1940, and then drive in a north-easterly direction to Antwerp, cutting the Allied front in two. All this was fantasy but Hitler insisted the attack would go ahead, despite protests from the commanders who would actually have to carry it out.

Allied intelligence was aware of the assembly of German reserves but believed they were intended as a counter-attack force against any future Allied advances. The Ardennes region was indeed one of the weakest parts of the Allied line, held by an unfortunate mix of resting veterans and inexperienced newcomers. The Allied commitment to advances to the north and south of the region also meant that there were few

reserves available to use elsewhere. Altogether the Germans assembled ten Panzer divisions, equipped with many of the newest heavy tanks, and a number of newly raised *Volksgrenadier* infantry units. Three armies were deployed; together they formed Field Marshal Walther Model's Army Group B.

INITIAL GERMAN GAINS

The Germans attacked on 16 December and achieved complete surprise. They quickly broke through the Allied line all along the attack front, while small groups of special forces penetrated deeper into Allied territory, spreading confusion and panic. A few Allied reinforcements were quickly sent to the area and they, and the survivors of the original front-line force, established themselves especially around the towns of St-Vith and Bastogne. They were both important road junctions, particularly vital for movement in an area of steep and densely wooded hillsides.

By the 19th the top Allied commanders were taking the situation in hand. All Allied attacks elsewhere were halted and new arrangements to deal with the threat established. Field Marshal Montgomery was put in charge of the Anglo-American forces north of the German advance, and General Omar Bradley of the US forces to the south. Part of Patton's US Third Army changed front with

Above: Men of US 75th Division advancing toward St-Vith during the Allied counter-attack in January 1945.

BODENPLATTE

The Luftwaffe planned a knock-out blow – Operation Bodenplatte – against Allied air bases in Belgium to accompany the Ardennes offensive. It was finally delivered on 1 January 1945 with something approaching 900 German aircraft taking part, many flown by novice pilots. They surprised a number of Allied airfields and destroyed about 150 aircraft, mostly on the ground, but about 300 of the German planes and many of the most experienced pilots were shot down. It was yet another serious defeat for the Luftwaffe.

BATTLE OF THE BULGE

The German plan for the Ardennes offensive was to split the Allied armies apart and capture their principal supply port, Antwerp.

astonishing speed and began attacking north to relieve Bastogne and reduce the bulge the Germans had now driven into the Allied line.

Up to this point bad weather had kept Allied air support to a minimum, but on the 22nd it cleared. The German supply system was already stretched; now both it and the front-line forces came under continuous attack. A few German troops almost reached the River Meuse by late on the 24th and would go no further. Their generals were already begging Hitler's permission to call off the attack (and being refused).

THE ALLIED RESPONSE

After an epic defence, Bastogne was relieved by Patton's advance on 26 December. Major attacks from the north of the Bulge began on 3 January, and it had largely been recovered by the middle of the month. The Germans lost about 100,000 men and most of the tanks used in the operation. Allied losses were similar in number but theirs could be replaced. Germany's could not.

Victory in the West and Italy

Allied commanders anticipated a hard struggle to conquer Germany. Instead, after they crossed the Rhine, German resistance collapsed within weeks. However, the great prize of Berlin was left for the Soviets to take.

After the disappointments of the autumn of 1944 and the hard fighting of the Battle of the Bulge at the turn of the year, the Allied commanders did not expect to finish the campaign against Germany easily. In particular they thought that crossing the Rhine against tough German opposition would be difficult, but events proved them wrong.

British and Canadian troops opened the Allied offensive at the north end of the line in early February, fighting a vicious battle through the Reichswald forest to close up to the Rhine. US Ninth Army on their southern flank was meant to join the attack shortly after but was delayed by extensive flooding, deliberately caused by the Germans. By early March, however, Ninth Army was on the

Above: Men of British Eighth Army near Ferrara during the final Allied attacks in Italy in April 1945.

move and had been joined by US First and Third Armies farther to the south still.

Within days the Allied troops had reached the Rhine everywhere north of Cologne, and on

7 March US First Army reached Remagen some 45km (28 miles) to the south.

Better still, the Americans captured the railway bridge over the river there before it could be destroyed by the retreating Germans, and immediately started rushing troops across. Finally, the last Allied armies, US Seventh and French First, overran almost all the remaining German-held territory west of the river by mid-month.

Montgomery's British forces made their long-planned assault crossing of the Rhine from late on the 23rd around Wesel, with much less difficulty than anticipated. Originally this had been conceived as the main Allied advance but the crossing at Remagen had been joined on the 22nd by another – by Third Army south of Mainz. Patton was determined to steal Monty's glory. A few days earlier General Eisenhower had already decided to modify Allied plans by strengthening these attacks south of the Ruhr.

ENCIRCLING THE RUHR

Hitler was still issuing his usual orders that there should be no retreat and fanatical resistance. However, the reality was that increasing numbers of German troops were now only too glad to surrender to the Western Allies

Left: American troops at the bridge at Remagen, the first crossing point over the Rhine captured by the Allies.

in order to keep themselves safe from the Russians. New Allied advances at the end of March encircled the whole Ruhr area and the troops there – over 300,000 strong – surrendered in mid-April.

By this stage Soviet troops were on the Oder, only 65km (40 miles) from Berlin and seemed well-placed to capture it. In mid-March Eisenhower therefore decided that his forces would not try to reach Berlin but would concentrate their advances farther south against a feared (though actually non-existent) National Redoubt that fanatical Nazis were supposedly building for a last stand in southern Germany.

In fact the Anglo-American armies were now advancing at speed all along the front, while the Soviets were not yet ready for their final drive to Berlin. US troops reached the Elbe west of the German capital in mid-April and halted there, with first contact with the Soviets coming a little to the south-west on the 25th at Torgau.

LAST BATTLES IN ITALY
After the capture of Rome in June 1944, Allied troops had been taken from Italy for the invasion of southern France. The remaining Allied units continued a slow advance into early 1945. In April they renewed their attacks, now with more success. German forces in Italy surrendered on 2 May, and on 4 May the advancing Allied troops linked up at the Brenner Pass with US Seventh Army coming down through Bavaria.

By early May most of what would become West Germany was in Anglo-American hands

and the formal surrenders began here, too. German forces in the north capitulated to Montgomery on the 4th, followed by a complete German surrender that was signed at Eisenhower's headquarters on the 7th.

Above: Tanks and troops of US Third Army crossing the Rhine near Koblenz on a pontoon bridge.

Below: An Allied M3 half track on the advance through the ruins of a German town in early 1945.

The Fall of Berlin

*In the last weeks of the war the ruin that Hitler had brought to Europe was visited
in yet a more terrible form on Berlin, as the Soviet armies rampaged through
the city above his bunker and across much of Germany.*

From the start, WWII had been a total war, prosecuted with the utmost violence and cruelty, and its final great battle saw this trend continue to the last. At the end of March 1945 General Eisenhower had told the Soviets that his forces would stop short of Berlin and make no attempt to capture the city. Stalin did not believe him and hurried forward the Red Army's preparations to get there first.

ODER BREAKTHROUGH

The Soviet attack began on 16 April with some 2.5 million men and a truly astonishing 16,000 artillery weapons deployed. The Germans had perhaps one million men, but many of them were over-age or very young. They had nothing like the scale of equipment of their enemies, and even when they did have tanks they had scarcely any fuel

---

KEY FACTS

PLACE: Berlin

DATE: 16 April–2 May 1945

OUTCOME: Soviet troops advanced from the River Oder to conquer Berlin; Hitler committed suicide.

---

for them. Even so, the initial Soviet attacks, by Zhukov's 1st Belorussian Front, against the Seelow Heights west of Küstrin failed to break through, in part because Army Group Vistula was now led by an acknowledged defensive expert, General Gotthard Heinrici.

However, by 20 April the German resistance had inevitably fallen apart. Zhukov's surge toward Berlin and round its

north side had also been joined by a major drive by Konev's 2nd Ukrainian Front over the Neisse a little to the south.

To ensure the fastest progress Stalin gave both his marshals permission to take Berlin, according to which got there first. Zhukov's troops reached the edges of the city on the 21st and the two fronts met to complete the encirclement west of Potsdam on the 25th. On the same day Konev's men made contact with US troops at Torgau on the Elbe to the south.

Over the next few days the Soviets fought their way from street to street and house to house. On 30 April they stormed the Reichstag building, only 400m (440yd) from Hitler's command bunker. On the 29th Hitler had named Admiral Dönitz as his successor and then killed himself. The fighting went on a little longer, but on 2 May the Soviet fronts linked up from north and south and the last of the garrison surrendered.

In the meantime the remaining troops of the German Ninth Army, part of the defence force on the Oder a couple of weeks before, were attacking desperately to the west to escape the Soviets and surrender to the Americans. They knew only too well the fate that probably would await them in Soviet captivity. Since the Soviets had

Left: Raising the Red Flag over Germany's parliament, the Reichstag.

Legend:
- Soviet attacks
- Anglo-American attacks
- Front line 15 Apr 1945
- Front line 25 Apr 1945
- Front line 6 May 1945
- German defence lines

MARSHAL IVAN KONEV

Konev (1897–1973) was a tough and competent Soviet commander who held senior posts throughout the war. He played a notable part as a front commander in the defence of Moscow in late 1941 but then, and later in his career, he was somewhat overshadowed by Zhukov, with whom he had a great rivalry. Konev's public reputation grew with his part in the Ukraine and Polish battles of 1943–4. In 1945 he shared in the conquest of Berlin, inevitably with Zhukov, but Konev finished the war off on his own by leading the capture of Prague.

BATTLE OF BERLIN

The Soviet advance from the Oder took only about three weeks to overwhelm Berlin.

entered Germany, their advance had been marked by a rampage of murder, rape and drunken looting, which now reached a terrible climax in and around the enemy capital.

GERMANY SURRENDERS

With Hitler dead, the end was certain. German troops in Italy surrendered on 2 May, in north Germany on 4 May and in south Germany on 5 May. On 7 May Dönitz's representatives signed the overall surrender at Eisenhower's HQ at Reims. Stalin suspiciously insisted that the signing be repeated late on the

Right: Soviet Josef Stalin tanks in front of the captured Reichstag.

8th in Berlin. The Western Allies, however, celebrated VE-Day (Victory in Europe) on the 8th, the Soviets on the 9th.

Even then the killing was not over. Some of the last German units holding out by late April were in Czechoslovakia. On 5

May the people of Prague rose against the Germans, who fought back fiercely. Over the next week Soviet units closed in from the east and north, and the final German force surrendered on the 13th. The war in Europe was finally over.

The Battle of Leyte Gulf
Japanese kamikaze pilots at a pre-mission ceremony.

Landing Craft and Amphibious Vehicles A wrecked Japanese landing barge on Saipan.

Submarines and Bombers
Admiral Lockwood aboard the submarine USS *Balao*.

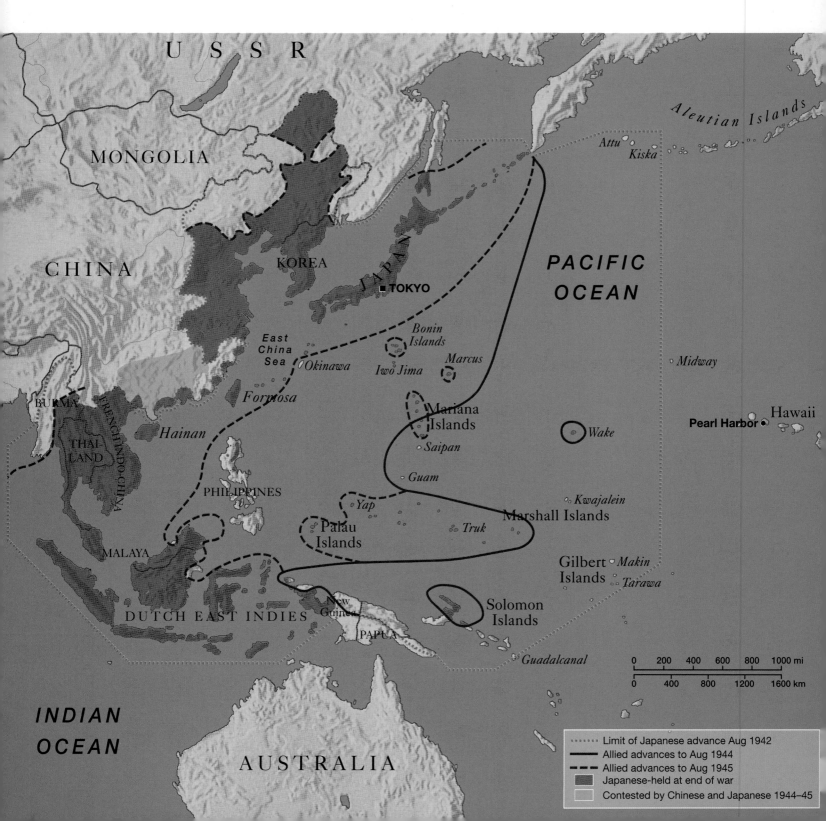

U S S R

MONGOLIA

CHINA

KOREA

JAPAN

■ TOKYO

Aleutian Islands

Attu

Kiska

PACIFIC
OCEAN

East
China
Sea

*Bonin
Islands*

Okinawa

Iwo Jima

Marcus

Midway

Formosa

BURMA

FRENCH INDO-CHINA

THAI-
LAND

Hainan

Mariana
Islands

Saipan

Wake

Pearl Harbor

Hawaii

PHILIPPINES

Guam

Yap

Palau
Islands

Truk

Kwajalein

Marshall Islands

MALAYA

Gilbert
Islands

Makin

Tarawa

DUTCH EAST INDIES

New
Guinea

PAPUA

Solomon
Islands

Guadalcanal

INDIAN
OCEAN

AUSTRALIA

| 0 | 200 | 400 | 600 | 800 | 1000 mi |

| 0 | 400 | 800 | 1200 | 1600 km |

.... Limit of Japanese advance Aug 1942
——— Allied advances to Aug 1944
- - - - Allied advances to Aug 1945
Japanese-held at end of war
Contested by Chinese and Japanese 1944–45

DESTRUCTION OF THE JAPANESE EMPIRE

By 1943 the vast expansion of America's military strength was taking effect. Despite large increases in its own war production Japan could not begin to compete. From relatively small beginnings in New Guinea and the Solomons, the Allied counter-offensive soon developed in pace and strength. The US Navy and Marines began their island-hopping advance across the Central Pacific and MacArthur's Allied South-west Pacific Command surged toward the Philippines. By mid-1944 a relentless submarine campaign was making Japan's vaunted empire practically useless to the homeland, which was itself coming under heavy bombing attack. On the Asian mainland Japan could still advance against weak Chinese forces, but plans to invade India from Burma had been smashed by the British–Indian Fourteenth Army.

The second half of 1944 and early 1945 saw the ring around Japan tighten with the fall of the Philippines, Iwo Jima and Okinawa. The desperate expedient of suicidal kamikaze attacks did little to slow the American advance. Allied plans for an invasion of Japan were well in hand by August 1945, when everything changed with the atom bomb attacks on Hiroshima and Nagasaki and the crushing Soviet offensive on mainland Asia. Japan's surrender followed within days.

Naval Bombers and Torpedo Aircraft A US Navy Curtiss SB2C Helldiver in flight.

Conquest of the Philippines US Navy landing ships unloading troops and supplies on Leyte.

The Japanese Surrender The mushroom cloud of an atomic explosion rises above Nagasaki.

New Guinea and the Solomons

*Japan's troops began paying the price for their reckless early-war conquests.
Garrisons were isolated and then either picked off or left to starve as the Allied
forces pushed past in their counter-offensive toward the Philippines.*

After the triumph at Midway, American strategists knew that they could move to the attack in the Pacific, but there was fierce debate on how to develop the counter-offensive. General MacArthur, now established in Australia at the head of the Allied South-west Pacific Command, argued forcibly for an advance through the Solomons and along the north coast of New Guinea toward eventual fulfilment of his promise to return to the Philippines.

Admiral Chester Nimitz, commanding the Pacific Ocean Areas from his base in Hawaii, wanted to advance via the island groups of the Central Pacific. Like MacArthur's, this was a strategy that favoured his own command and his own service, the US Navy, but in truth it was also likely to be more direct and economical in casualties and material. However, American resources were becoming so ample that both plans could be

Above: Stuart tanks leading a search for Japanese positions, New Georgia Island, August 1943.

pursued. Indeed it would have been very difficult politically for the President and his advisers, with whom the decision ultimately rested, to have chosen one strategy exclusively.

AIR SUPERIORITY

All the Allied advances were based on air power, an area in which they were clearly superior by the end of 1942. This was well demonstrated in the Battle of the Bismarck Sea in the first days of March 1943. A Japanese convoy had sailed from Rabaul to reinforce their forward positions on New Guinea around Lae but was attacked en route. A dozen ships were sunk and around 4,000 soldiers drowned.

The attacks were made possible by code-breaking information, which would play a vital part throughout the remainder of the campaign. Time and again the Allied forces would attack weakly defended locations and quickly build air bases to ensure dominance over any stronger Japanese forces nearby.

Major Japanese positions were neutralized by air attacks and then in effect ignored, left to "wither on the vine" while the Allied advance moved on elsewhere. This technique was even applied to the principal Japanese strongholds of Rabaul and Kavieng, which eventually were left isolated and impotent (though early plans had provided for their capture).

NEW GUINEA

In the first phase of the advance the Japanese were drawn forward, by air landings and naval attacks by Australian and American forces, toward Wau and Salamaua – and then kept off balance by other forces leap-

Left: B-25 bombers of US Fifth Air Force attacking a Japanese airfield on New Guinea, February 1943.

frogging on to the Markham Valley and Huon Peninsula areas. In the second phase, in April–May 1944, landings at Aitape and Hollandia isolated tens of thousands of Japanese troops around Wewak. The final landings on western New Guinea and nearby islands established bases to support the Marianas and Philippines operations, which were to follow.

THE SOLOMONS

Again the same techniques were followed in the Solomons campaign. This was most clearly seen in the landings on Bougainville, which began on 1 November 1943. The island had a garrison of some 60,000 Japanese troops concentrated in the south around Buin. Instead of attacking directly, US Marines landed 120km (75 miles) away on the east coast at Empress Augusta Bay. By the time the Japanese had crossed the jungle to the Allied beachhead it was easily strong enough to repel their attacks.

Although fighting on Bougainville continued to the end of the war, by then being conducted on the Allied side mainly by Australian forces, the

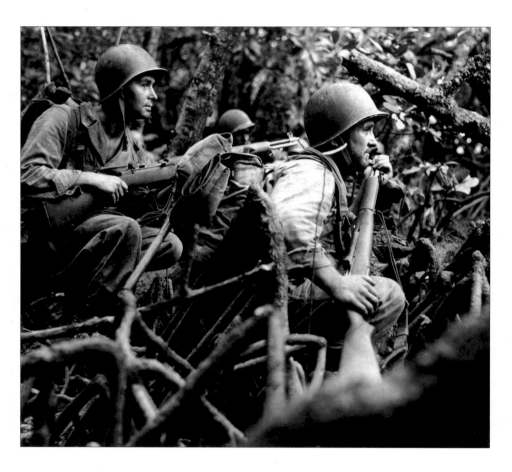

starving Japanese garrison, like others in the region, was contributing nothing of value to Japan's war effort.

Above: US Army troops advance cautiously through dense jungle on Vella Lavella Island in the New Georgia group, September 1943.

Above: Australian troops in a landing craft shortly before the attack on Lae, September 1943.

GENERAL DOUGLAS MACARTHUR

MacArthur (1880–1964) was the top US Army general in the Pacific throughout the war. He commanded the American and local forces in the Philippines in 1941 but was quickly defeated by the first Japanese attacks. MacArthur was ordered to leave and take over a new Allied South-west Pacific Command, which he led successfully in the New Guinea campaign until the return to the Philippines in 1944–5. Like many top commanders, he was a great egotist and self-publicist, but he was nonetheless also a talented and effective general.

Below: General MacArthur in the Philippines in early 1945 after his promotion to General of the Army.

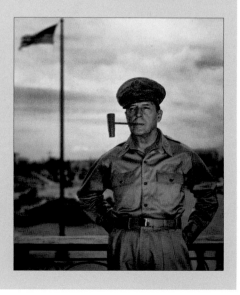

The Central Pacific Campaign

From late 1943, the US Navy and Marines fought a new kind of war across the Central Pacific, characterized by the description "island-hopping", which relied as much on novel methods of logistical support as the efforts of the combat forces.

In 1943 the US Navy took 15 fleet or light aircraft carriers into service, but the Japanese commissioned only 1. The USA also out-produced Japan by 4 to 1 in submarines, roughly 10 to 1 in destroyers and by similar wide margins in every other class of munitions.

Nor was Japan husbanding its resources well. The already diminished cadre of trained carrier aircrews was further decimated in the early part of the year by being deployed on land in the Solomons and New Guinea. Training and improved

Right: The carrier USS *Lexington* refuelling at sea during the Tarawa operation, November 1943.

Below: US Marines lie dead amid the devastation and debris on the beach at Tarawa.

KEY FACTS

PLACE: Tarawa Atoll, Gilbert Islands

DATE: 20–3 November 1943

OUTCOME: Japanese garrison wiped out despite heavy American casualties.

equipment (notably better aircraft and radar) were also offsetting Japan's previous qualitative advantage in some areas, in air combat and naval night fighting, for example.

Even with potential combat superiority, the US forces still had the problem of distance to overcome: the US Pacific Fleet's base at Pearl Harbor was 3,200km (2,000 miles) from the West Coast; the Solomon Islands 14,500km (9,000 miles) from California; Australia still farther. To keep troops, ships and aircraft fed, fuelled and armed over such vast distances required a huge logistic effort.

The solution was a new type of naval organization, the fleet train, including tankers and other kinds of supply ship, so that combat vessels could be replenished at sea during assault operations far from any base. Then a range of new bases was improvised by rapidly building shore installations and installing floating docks in various previously tranquil Pacific lagoons – like Ulithi in the Caroline Islands (an important base from September 1944).

THE GILBERT ISLANDS
The first step was to make landings from 20 November 1943 on the Tarawa and Makin Atolls in the Gilbert Islands. The Makin landings, mainly on Butaritari Island, were fiercely contested, but the US Army troops wiped out all resistance by the 23rd.

Above: US Marines ready to move inland from their landing beach, Eniwetok, February 1944.

However, Betio Island, the main target in the Tarawa Atoll, was a different matter.

Only 3km (2 miles) long and nowhere wider than 800m (880yd), none of Betio is more than 3m (9ft) above sea level. By November 1943 the 4,800-strong Japanese garrison had built a formidable network of bunkers and gun positions that largely survived the preliminary bombardments. The landing force, principally the 2nd US Marine Division, also lacked information on the depth of water in the lagoon and over the coral reef. For these reasons some 1,500 of the initial 5,000-man assault force became casualties on the first day, but the survivors held on. By the 23rd the only living Japanese were a

handful of wounded, plus a few captured Korean labourers. US Marine casualties were over 1,000 dead and 2,000 wounded.

THE MARSHALL ISLANDS

The next stage was to seize control of the Marshall Islands. These were not as strongly fortified as was feared, although there were significant air forces deployed across a number of islands. These were gradually worn down from late 1943 by carrier attacks and land-based aircraft from the Gilberts.

On 31 January 1944 US troops began landings on Kwajalein, Roi-Namur and Majuro. The fiercest fighting was on Kwajalein, but by 4 February the 8,700-strong garrison had fought virtually to the last man, inflicting 370 dead on the attackers. Later in February Eniwetok was also captured. At the same time Japan's greatest

SEABEES

The Seabees were in effect combat engineers of the US Navy, working and, when necessary, fighting on land. They were first organized from late 1941 and their popular name derives from the initials "CB" for Construction Battalions, which was their official designation. At first all the men were volunteer civilian craftsmen or engineers, though draftees joined later. They served in all theatres but mainly in the Pacific. Typically they would land very shortly after the initial assault force and immediately begin work on airstrips and other base facilities. Without their efforts the island-hopping strategy would have been impossible.

Above: Seabees setting up communications facilities on one of the Gilbert Islands.

overseas base, at Truk in the Caroline Islands, was heavily hit by the US carrier forces. The USA's relentless progress would continue without respite for the Japanese.

The Marianas Campaign

The capture of the Marianas and Japan's crushing defeat in the naval Battle of the Philippine Sea ruptured the perimeter of its empire. The southern areas were being cut off as the war approached ever nearer to the Home Islands.

Although by mid-1944 the outer reaches of the Japanese Empire were increasingly helpless in the face of American advances, Japan's leaders still dreamed of setting all right by victory in a decisive naval battle. Their plan, code-named A-Go, was to mount a series of attacks by carrier and land-based aircraft to defeat the main American forces.

Unfortunately, not only did the American fleet have twice as many carrier aircraft (950:470)

Below: US troops in action on Saipan. The landings were made by the 2nd and 4th Marine Divisions and the 27th (Army) Infantry Division.

Above: Admiral Ozawa commanded Japanese naval forces in the Battle of the Philippine Sea and the carrier decoy force at Leyte Gulf.

but – in addition to the by now usual American advantages in code breaking and intelligence generally – the A-Go plan had been passed to them after being taken from a Japanese officer's crashed aircraft by guerrillas in the Philippines.

SAIPAN, TINIAN, GUAM

On 15 June two US Marine divisions landed on Saipan to set the land fighting in motion. Saipan had the strongest Japanese garrison in the area, some 27,000 men, but by 9 July the last effective resistance was destroyed. The landings on nearby Tinian began on 24 July; here the 6,200-strong garrison had been wiped out by 1 August. Guam was also captured from its 19,000-man garrison after fierce fighting, with the landings beginning on 21 July; organized Japanese resistance ceased by 10 August.

The Japanese garrisons all fought virtually to the last man. The American forces, mainly US Marines, lost some 5,000 dead. By then, however, the A-Go battle had long since been fought.

BATTLE OF THE PHILIPPINE SEA

When the preliminary American air attacks on the islands started, Admiral Toyoda Soemu, Commander of the Japanese Combined Fleet, gave the order for A-Go to begin. Almost immediately things went wrong

Above: The carrier *Zuikaku* and several destroyers trying to dodge US air attacks, 20 July 1944. *Zuikaku* was hit but not sunk.

for the Japanese. As the fleet approached it was spotted by US submarines. At the same time American air attacks destroyed most of the Japanese aircraft force on the Mariana Islands themselves, as well as those on Iwo Jima and other islands that were meant to be sent to the Marianas. Crucially, the local commander on the Marianas hid the bad news from the fleet's tactical commander, Admiral Ozawa Jisaburo, who believed that the American forces were being worn down as he approached.

The one remaining Japanese advantage was in the range of both their combat and reconnaissance aircraft. It enabled them to find the American carriers and send off their strikes first, in the morning of 19 June. In all Ozawa sent off 4 strikes involving some 370 aircraft in the course of the day; about two-thirds were shot down while other Japanese planes were destroyed over Guam. Only one American ship was hit by a bomb and only 29 American aircraft lost.

Japanese aircraft and their hastily trained crews could no longer compete with the American pilots and anti-aircraft gunners, who called the day's events the "Great Marianas Turkey Shoot". Even worse for the Japanese, two of their largest carriers – the *Taiho* and *Shokaku* – were torpedoed and sunk by American submarines.

Despite all this, Ozawa tried to continue the battle, believing the optimistic reports that were still reaching him. On 20 June American reconnaissance did not fix the Japanese position until well into the afternoon when some 130 bombers and 85 fighters were sent to attack, even though the American commanders knew that their pilots would have to return to the carriers after dark. Another Japanese carrier was sunk and 3 more damaged for the loss of 20 American aircraft. Over 70 craft were lost while returning to their carriers, but most of the crews were picked up.

By contrast hardly any crew members of the more than 400 Japanese aircraft lost in the battle were saved. Thus, the biggest ever carrier battle also marked the effective demise of the Japanese carrier force. They still had ships but hardly any trained crews to fly from them.

ADMIRAL CHESTER NIMITZ

Nimitz (1885–1966) commanded the US Pacific Fleet from a few days after Pearl Harbor until the end of the war. His leadership, more than that of any other commander, was responsible for the series of crushing defeats inflicted on Japan and the transformation of the US Navy from the low ebb of December 1941 to absolute dominance in 1944–5. His leadership was probably best seen in the difficult times of 1942, when his able use of intelligence led directly to the first great success at Midway.

Above: Fleet Admiral Chester Nimitz pictured in 1945.

Burma, 1943–4

The retreat in Burma in 1942 was the longest in British history, but by mid-1944 the British–Indian Fourteenth Army had inflicted what was then Japan's worst-ever defeat on land in the Battles of Imphal and Kohima.

Japan's aim in attacking Burma in 1942 was to cut the vital Burma Road supply route to China and, in due course, to advance onward to India. British intentions were to defend India and in time recover Burma and later Malaya, while US leaders were less interested in victory in Burma for its own sake than as a means of reopening a supply route to China and the development there of powerful attacks on Japan. In the end, though Japan's advance on India was thrown back in 1944, Burma's position far down the Allied priority list helped ensure neither British nor American plans would come fully to fruition.

Burma's monsoon season made large-scale military operations impossible each year from

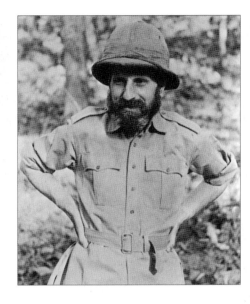

Above: Orde Wingate led the Chindits in 1943, but died in 1944 during a second Chindit operation.

late May to early November. By later in 1942 Allied forces had been rebuilt sufficiently after the debacle earlier in the year to attempt a modest offensive in the coastal Arakan region. After several months of fighting, the Japanese recaptured most of the ground briefly gained – an outcome which confirmed that they still held the upper hand tactically and psychologically in jungle battle.

THE CHINDITS

The only other offensive move possible in that period was an entirely novel "long-range penetration" operation by a force called the Chindits, led by the charismatic (and barely sane) Brigadier Orde Wingate. Supplied from the air, they operated well behind Japanese lines, cutting communications and attacking bases for some weeks before being ordered to return to India. Wingate was lionized by Churchill; he and his men were celebrated in the press as having shown that the Japanese were not invincible in the jungle. Reality was different: a third of the force was lost, hardly any of the survivors were fit for future operations and their attacks achieved nothing.

The real way forward was shown by another series of Arakan battles in late 1943–early 1944. The British advance there was intended as part of a general Allied offensive, while the Japanese planned their own attack as a preliminary to a drive into India in the Imphal area, far inland to the north-east. In the event part of the British force was surrounded for a time, a circumstance that had often led to

Below: A British 25pdr (88mm) gun position in the Burmese jungle.

Right: Japanese and Indian National Army men during the Imphal campaign.

defeat in the past. Now better-trained, the troops stood their ground (with the benefit of air supply) and simply out-fought the Japanese. Much of this success was down to General Bill Slim, in command of the British forces in Burma, Fourteenth Army, since October 1943.

IMPHAL AND KOHIMA

A similar pattern emerged on the main inland battle front, after much hard fighting. Under the codename U-Go, the Japanese planned to advance into India with attacks led by General Mutaguchi Renya's Fifteenth Army. Slim and other British commanders expected a Japanese attack but were caught by surprise by the speed of their advance. As a result a small force was surrounded at Kohima and a larger one at Imphal on 4–5 April. Once again the plan was to hold firm with air support until relief troops fought their way through from the north.

The siege of Kohima was broken by late April after a vicious close-quarter battle in and around the town. It took until well into June for the advance to link up with the Imphal garrison and another month before the Japanese finally retreated. While Slim's men had been receiving thousands of tons of supplies and substantial reinforcements by

Below: British troops serving with the 19th Indian Division in action with 3in (76.2mm) mortars near Imphal.

air throughout the battle, the Japanese had been operating on a logistical shoestring; many were now starving. They lost about 60,000 casualties, more than half of them dead, compared to some 17,000 British and Indian killed and wounded.

THE INDIAN NATIONAL ARMY

This force, recruited mainly from Indian Army prisoners of war captured in Malaya in 1942, was formed to support the cause of Indian independence by fighting with the Japanese against the British. It had various changes of leaders and organization but from mid-1943 was led by Subhas Chandra Bose and had a maximum strength of about 20,000. It was never fully trusted by the Japanese and was mainly used in small detachments. INA troops fought (but usually not very effectively) in various battles in Burma from early 1944 to the end of the war.

The Battle of Leyte Gulf

The three separate engagements comprising the Battle of Leyte Gulf together make up the largest naval battle in history. Despite their huge superiority, the US forces only just escaped terrible losses to the Leyte invasion fleet.

As the US advance gathered pace in mid-1944, commanders argued about how to attack Japan. General MacArthur felt the Philippines should be recaptured, but US Navy leaders favoured Formosa (now Taiwan) as the next target. In the end, landings on Leyte were planned for 20 October, with the main Philippine island of Luzon to be attacked at the end of the year.

THE JAPANESE PLAN

Japan still had many big-gun ships, including the *Yamato* and *Musashi*, the largest battleships ever built. Japan's admirals also

---

KEY FACTS

PLACE: Three separate battles among and near the Philippine Islands

---

DATE: 24–5 October 1944

OUTCOME: Americans narrowly avoided a disaster to win a major victory.

THE BATTLE OF LEYTE GULF
The Japanese approach and the three Leyte Gulf battles, within the Philippine Islands complex.

---

wanted an all-out battle in which these ships might turn the tide of the war. The Japanese naval air arm was no longer powerful: it had aircraft carriers but few trained crews or planes. Admiral Toyoda's Sho-Go plan (Operation Victory) called for carriers to divert the main American strength to the north, with most of the heavy ships attacking the vulnerable US landing fleet from the west through various channels between the Philippine Islands.

The US landings on Leyte began on 20 October. The main Japanese force, Force A, sailed from Borneo on the 22nd. US submarines sank two cruisers and reported Force A's move the next day. On 24 October the American carrier *Princeton* was sunk by land-based aircraft.

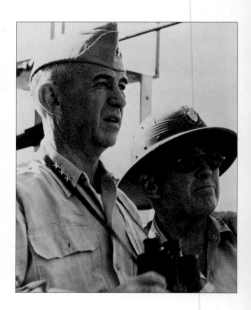

Above: Admiral Thomas Kinkaid (left) and General Walter Krueger, commander of Sixth Army on Leyte.

Above: The carrier USS *Princeton* on fire and sinking, 24 October.

Force A was attacked by US carrier aircraft in the Sibuyan Sea; the *Musashi* was sunk by bombs and torpedoes. Admiral Kurita Takeo ordered a brief turn away because of these attacks.

HALSEY'S MISTAKE

The two main US naval forces were Admiral William Halsey's Third Fleet, including the main carrier force, Task Force 38; and Admiral Thomas Kinkaid's Seventh Fleet of transport and support vessels. Halsey now assumed (incorrectly) that Force A had retreated for good and (correctly) that Kinkaid's shore-bombardment ships could cope with the Japanese southern force. He therefore felt free to take his main force north against the Japanese carriers.

Thus, in the early hours of the 25th, the old battleships of the Seventh Fleet triumphed in a night gun and torpedo battle in the Surigao Strait; two Japanese battleships were among the vessels sunk. Now, after earlier abortive strikes, the Japanese carriers in the north had barely a couple of dozen aircraft left between them to face the ten full-strength carriers of TF 38. Three Japanese carriers and

Below: The destroyer *Akizuki*, sunk during the Battle of Cape Engaño.

several other ships were sunk during the 25th in the Battle of Cape Engaño.

More would have been sent down but part of the US attack had to be called off by emergency messages from the fleet off Leyte, suddenly facing Force A. This should easily have had the gun-power to brush aside the weak escort carriers and destroyers that stood between it and the virtually defenceless invasion transports.

Instead resolute American defence and a developing fuel shortage persuaded Kurita to turn away feebly after an inconclusive combat, known as the Battle of Samar. The various Japanese forces suffered further losses during their retreats. When all were counted, what might have been an American disaster thus turned into another catastrophe for Japan's fleet.

KAMIKAZE ATTACKS

By 1944 numerous Japanese garrisons had made desperate suicidal attacks as a last resort but suicide kamikaze attacks, from October 1944, became a deliberate first-choice tactic. The first organized kamikaze attack was on 21 October off Leyte; the cruiser HMAS *Australia* was badly damaged. The first kamikazes used standard fighters, but aircraft fitted with heavy bombs were later employed along with various purpose-built craft, including piloted flying bombs, explosive motor boats, manned torpedoes and midget submarines. Around 500 kamikaze air attacks were made during the Philippine campaign and perhaps 2,000 during the fighting on Okinawa in 1945.

Above: Kamikaze pilots are given their ceremonial headbands.

Conquest of the Philippines

When General MacArthur had left the Philippines in 1942, he had pledged: "I shall return." He landed on Leyte to fulfil that pledge in October 1944, but Japanese forces were still holding out on Luzon when the war ended almost a year later.

The planned Allied landings on Leyte in the south-west of the Philippine archipelago were hurriedly brought forward when aircraft carrier attacks suggested that the island might be relatively lightly defended. This proved to be a false hope, but in the end the established pattern of Pacific engagements was repeated, with the American forces gradually wearing down a tough and determined defending force.

THE BATTLE FOR LEYTE

General Walter Krueger's Sixth Army landed some 130,000 troops on the east coast of Leyte

Below: The material strength Japan could never approach. Massed US LSTs land supplies on Leyte.

Above: General MacArthur (in sunglasses) wades ashore on Leyte on his return to the Philippines.

on 20 October 1944, the first day of the operation. General MacArthur was also present, dramatically wading ashore from a landing craft (and then typically repeating the process

for the benefit of the assembled press cameramen). The initial Japanese force on Leyte was some 20,000 strong but General Yamashita, recently appointed as Japan's top commander in the Philippines, sent some 50,000 reinforcements to the island, though these took significant casualties and lost much equipment in transit.

Although the Japanese Navy was in the end decisively defeated in its attempts to intervene in the Battle of Leyte Gulf, the fighting on land was bitterly contested. Ultimately the Japanese had no answer to the American land and air firepower and organized resistance came to an end by late December. Casualties were as disproportionate as ever – over 60,000 Japanese dead compared to 3,600 Americans.

By then the US Eighth Army, commanded by General Robert Eichelberger, was also involved in the fight, having begun landings on the lightly defended Mindoro Island on the 15th of that month. As usual, they quickly built airfields to support future operations.

LIBERATING LUZON

General Yamashita had about a quarter of a million men left on Luzon by the end of the year, but inevitably they were greatly dispersed across the island's substantial area and were not well armed or equipped. Therefore, Yamashita decided not to

Above: An American casualty is taken for treatment amid the wreckage of Manila, February 1945.

Above: A US M10 Tank Destroyer in action in the infantry-support role on Leyte in late 1944.

contest in any great strength whatever landing beaches the Americans selected, but rather to retire gradually into the mountainous interior and hold out there for as long as possible.

On 9 January 1945 General MacArthur sent Sixth Army ashore in Lingayen Gulf. Kamikaze and conventional air attacks caused some damage to the landing fleet en route, but soon the few surviving Japanese aircraft were flown out to Formosa (Taiwan) and elsewhere.

TOWARD MANILA

As the Japanese invaders had in 1942, the US forces soon pushed south toward Manila, the capital. Here, in an exception to Yamashita's overall plan, the Japanese forces chose to stand and fight. The battle for

Manila lasted for a month, from early February to 3 March. Although MacArthur forbade air attacks, what the artillery bombardments and ground combat did not destroy, the Japanese blew up or set on fire. The city was flattened and about 1,000 Americans and 16,000 Japanese died in the battle along with probably 100,000 local civilians.

Operations on Luzon and elsewhere in the Philippines continued for the rest of the war, with organized Japanese forces gradually being confined in ever smaller and more remote areas. Filipino guerrillas, who had been active to some extent during the Japanese occupation, played an increasingly important role alongside the Americans in these operations. However, Yamashita still had 50,000 men under his command when he surrendered in August.

Right: A battery of 105mm (4.13in) howitzers shelling the Intramuros area of Manila in February 1945.

China's War

China lost more casualties in the war than any other nation apart from the Soviet Union, and the war between China and Japan was the longest of the series of conflicts that made up WWII.

The war in China was not a simple contest between two sides, as it was in most other areas of the conflict. By the late 1930s even as the Chinese Nationalist government of Jiang Jieshi (or Chiang Kai-shek in the then usual English spelling) was being pushed out of large areas of northern and coastal China, it was also coming into conflict with the growing power of the Chinese Communists, who were led by Mao Zedong (Mao Tse-tung).

INTERNAL STRUGGLES
In addition to these forces, and the million and a half Japanese troops in China and Manchuria by late 1941, were the significant armies of the puppet regimes set up by the Japanese and various local groupings of shifting loyalty. After Japan's

Below: Mao Zedong inspecting men of the Communist Eighth Route Army in Shensi province in 1944.

Above: Chinese Nationalist troops like these fought in Burma in 1944–5 to open the Ledo Road supply route.

attack in 1937, there was an official truce between the Nationalists and Communists, but in fact there was continued fighting between their forces at a local level. In the period up to December 1941 China's Communists were also successful in greatly expanding their organization in supposedly Japanese-controlled areas.

After Pearl Harbor, the Western Allies hoped, and the USA's leaders believed, that large and efficient Chinese Nationalist armies could be created and would play a major role in defeating Japan. However, for their parts Jiang and Mao were aware of two things: that there would one day be a showdown between them, and that Japan would be defeated by the USA without their aid and forced to leave China. This knowledge governed their conduct throughout the war.

The Communists would be more active in opposing the Japanese: in part for the credit they knew would increase their popularity among the Chinese people; and in part by default because the areas where they were building up their strength were also the areas where the Japanese were most active.

Jiang's position at the head of the Nationalist movement depended on his personal control over the army. Removing corruption and professionalizing it (as his American advisers, led by General Joseph Stilwell, wanted) would have jeopardized this control, so it was not done. Instead of being employed against the Japanese, American supplies were largely used, or held for later use, against the Communists.

By 1941 Japan's advances in China had mostly come to a halt. From then until 1944 the Japanese made few significant forward moves. Although Japan had forces deployed across large swathes of China, they did not actually hold much more than the major cities and the links between them. They fought repeated "anti-bandit" campaigns in the countryside, plundering and destroying as they went. During the war years the Japanese-controlled areas came under increasing Communist influence – most of the "bandits" were in fact Communist guerrillas.

JAPANESE OFFENSIVES

There was one significant Japanese offensive in 1942 after some of the Doolittle raiders had flown on to China following their attack on Tokyo. Various Chinese and American air bases were captured and in all perhaps a quarter of a million

Below: Chongqing, the Chinese Nationalists' wartime capital, after a Japanese air attack in May 1939.

Chinese were killed, a significant proportion of them by biological weapons.

By 1944 the USA had built up its Fourteenth Air Force in China. Its attacks within China (and the first raids on Japan itself that followed) provoked a major Japanese attack, notably in south China – the Ichi-Go Offensive from April that year. The Nationalist forces facing

Above: A US C-46 flying supplies on the difficult "Over the Hump" route from India to China.

this advance collapsed and the American air bases were easily overrun. The Chinese did regain some ground in the far south in 1945, but by then no one believed that China had much part to play in finally defeating Japan.

Victory in Burma, 1944–5

Fourteenth Army's series of brilliant victories continued from late 1944 to the end of the war. The successes at Meiktila and Mandalay ensured that Burma would be almost completely liberated by May 1945.

Although any Japanese thoughts of invading India had been crushed at Imphal in the first half of 1944, the Allied aims of opening a road to China and recovering Burma were still to be fulfilled. British, Indian and other British Empire troops of Fourteenth Army would make the main advance into central Burma, as well as a secondary move along the coast. At the same time a combination of Chinese, American and British troops fought farther north and inland to create the land supply route to China.

THE LEDO ROAD

US leaders, including General Joseph Stilwell (the USA's top soldier in China until October 1944) believed that the Chinese Nationalists could play a major role in defeating Japan, if only they could be adequately equipped by the Allies. Although great efforts had been made to fly supplies "Over the Hump" of the mountain ranges between India and China, truly significant quantities could only be delivered by land.

The route chosen started at Ledo, the north-eastern end of India's rail system, and then ran southward into Japanese-held territory to link with the old Burma Road, which had supplied China before Pearl Harbor. Construction began in late 1942, accompanied by advances to clear the Japanese out of the way. The road was finally opened in January 1945.

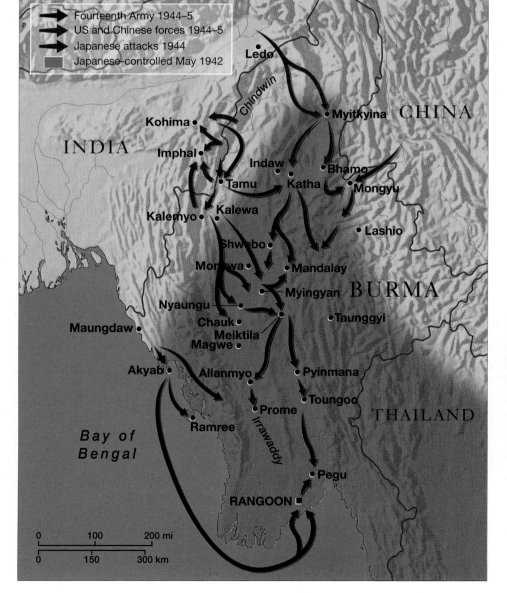

Below: British infantrymen watch Indian Army Sherman tanks approaching Meiktila, March 1945.

BURMA CAMPAIGN, 1943–5
Japan's defeats at Imphal and Kohima and the Allied offensive to liberate Burma.

Above: British troops crossing the River Chindwin at the start of their advance in late 1944.

The main battles in this sector were fought from late 1943 to August 1944, with the fighting being especially fierce around the town of Myitkyina. The Allied forces involved included the so-called Chinese Army in India, an American formation known as Merrill's Marauders and a second Chindit expedition that was much larger than the first.

SLIM'S MASTERPIECE

British leaders had a far more jaundiced (and as it turned out more realistic) view of what the Chinese Nationalists might contribute to the Allied war effort, preferring instead to advance in central Burma and plan seaborne operations farther south later.

Although the Japanese had substantially rebuilt their forces in Burma after the Imphal disaster, they were now clearly outmatched. The men of Fourteenth Army described themselves as the "forgotten army" because of their position far from home and well down the Allied priority list. However, they were in no doubt that the quality of their training, tactics and weaponry made them more than the equal of the Japanese in combat. They also had lavish air support and, above all, in General Slim, a resourceful and totally trusted commander.

When the advance began in late 1944, a deception scheme helped convince the Japanese that Mandalay (the traditional capital of Burma) was the Allied target. Instead General Slim's main plan was to capture the vital communications centre of Meiktila to the south, which was taken in early March. The force at Meiktila was isolated for several weeks by Japanese counter-attacks, but by late March these had been defeated – and the relentless pressure from other parts of Fourteenth Army had also taken Mandalay.

The Japanese were now in all-out retreat, though still capable of fighting tough rear-guard actions on occasion. With the monsoon season fast approaching, a seaborne attack on Rangoon was sent in. This

Above: General Slim in characteristic resolute pose.

took the city (which had been evacuated by the Japanese) shortly before Fourteenth Army arrived from the north.

The Japanese troops defending the coastal region were now cut off and trying to escape to the east. In the last fighting of the campaign before Japan finally surrendered, thousands of these men were killed at the cost of little more than a handful of Allied casualties.

Iwo Jima and Okinawa

The landings on these two islands were the last major operations planned before the invasion of the main parts of the Japanese homeland. Despite their disparity in size and terrain, both saw ferocious battles before the American forces gained control.

By 1945 American planners were clear that winning the war depended on taking bases from which the invasion of Japan could be mounted and supported. Iwo Jima offered airfields within fighter range of Tokyo; Okinawa had base and harbour areas suitable for supporting the vast force needed for the final invasion operations.

IWO JIMA

No more than a dot on the map of the Pacific, closer up Iwo Jima island is pear-shaped, 8km (5 miles) long and a maximum of 3km (2 miles) wide. In 1945

KEY FACTS – OKINAWA

PLACE: Okinawa, Ryukyu Islands

DATE: 1 April–21 June 1945

OUTCOME: US forces captured a final base for the invasion of Japan after very heavy casualties on both sides.

THE CAPTURE OF OKINAWA
The Japanese forces chose to defend only the south of the island in strength.

---

it had three airstrips but was mostly barren volcanic rock, with a 150m (500ft) extinct volcano, Mount Suribachi, at the southern end. In 1945 it was also perhaps the most heavily fortified area in the history of warfare, with a garrison of 21,000 men under General Kuribayashi Tadamichi, prepared to defend it to the last.

Kuribayashi's defences survived the extensive preliminary air and sea bombardment – he planned to let the attackers land before opening fire and revealing his positions. The landings began on 19 February with some 30,000 US Marines of V Amphibious Corps going ashore on the first day. Soon the Marines were being hit from all directions from the complex of trenches, tunnels and other strong points, which riddled the island. The result of the fighting was never in doubt, but the battle was vicious and bloody.

Above: A rocket-armed landing ship – LSM(R) – bombarding the Okinawa beaches, 1 April 1945.

Right: Smoke rises above Iwo Jima as US Marine amphibians approach the shore.

It took until 26 March to wipe out the defenders and cost the Marines almost 6,000 dead and over 17,000 wounded. By then, however, P-51 Mustang fighters were already operating from the island and its airfields were also providing emergency landing grounds for the B-29 force flying from the Marianas.

OKINAWA

The next target was a different and much bigger proposition. Although Okinawa is 560km (350 miles) from the nearest of the main Japanese Home Islands, it is part of "mainland" Japan (as is Iwo Jima). It would therefore be fiercely defended.

The Thirty-second Army defending the island, under the command of General Ushijima Mitsuru, was 120,000 strong. He had no intention of fighting on the beaches, for he had too much respect for American firepower.

Below: A kamikaze about to strike (and lightly damage) the battleship *Missouri* off Okinawa, 17 April 1945.

Instead he concentrated his troops in a relatively small but heavily fortified area of the south of the island, where the broken terrain would aid the defence in every way.

In all some half a million US troops and over 1,200 warships (including a significant British contingent) took part in the attack on Okinawa and various smaller islands nearby.

The naval forces suffered a blizzard of kamikaze attacks that sunk or damaged over 400 ships but never seriously disrupted Allied plans. The giant battleship *Yamato* was used as a suicide vessel, sailing from Japan with only enough fuel to reach Okinawa – it was sent to the bottom by air attacks on 7 April before it even came close.

The American landings had begun on 1 April and overran the northern three-quarters of the island by the middle of the month with relative ease. By then much harder fighting had started on the so-called Shuri Line to the south. It took two more months of vicious close-quarter battle before Japanese resistance ceased.

The US forces lost 12,500 dead on land and at sea and 35,000 wounded – frightening totals, considering the much bigger task of invading Japan itself that was in prospect.

However, the cost on the Japanese side was immense. Almost all the garrison troops were killed, as well as numerous civilians. Many more civilians committed suicide. As a final horror, among these were hundreds of children killed by their parents, who did not want them to suffer the brutalities that they had been told the Americans would commit.

Above: American troops riding up to the battlefront aboard a Sherman tank, Okinawa, 5 May 1945.

The Japanese Surrender

Japan had already suffered greatly by August 1945, but then came a succession of hammer blows: the atomic attacks on Hiroshima and Nagasaki and the Soviet declaration of war and subsequent crushing land offensive in Manchuria.

Ever since the Casablanca Conference in January 1943 the official Anglo-American policy was to seek the unconditional surrender of Japan. At that mid-war period, facing the prospect of a longer struggle to close in on Japan than in fact transpired, both the USA and Britain were keen to persuade the Soviets to join the war in the Far East. With offers of territorial and other concessions, Stalin duly promised at the Teheran Conference in late 1943 to declare war on Japan shortly after the war in Europe had been won.

When the Allied leaders met again at Potsdam in July 1945 much had changed: Hitler was dead in the ruins of nearby Berlin; Japan was far nearer to defeat in a shorter time than had once seemed possible; and on

Below: The centre of Hiroshima. Only a few stoutly constructed buildings still stand after the attack.

Above: The distinctive atomic mushroom cloud forms above the devastated city of Nagasaki.

the day before the conference started, the world's first nuclear bomb was tested in New Mexico. News of its power was rushed to the new US President Harry Truman and the British leaders at Potsdam.

The Japanese government had already begun making peace feelers through its

embassy in Moscow but it was clear from these that they wanted guarantees that Emperor Hirohito's position would not be at risk. The Allies could not accept this, feeling that to do so might be taken as a sign of weakness, which would encourage prolonged resistance.

Instead they issued the "Potsdam Declaration", which mentioned nothing about the Emperor but merely repeated the demand for unconditional surrender, threatening unspecified "utter destruction" if the demand was not met. In the meantime Stalin was officially told (though he already knew through his spies) that the USA had a new and powerful weapon ready for use against Japan and confirmed that he would soon be ready to attack Japan.

When the Japanese Prime Minister, Admiral Suzuki Kantaro, replied publicly to the declaration he said he would not comment on it for the moment; but he was misunderstood as saying that Japan would ignore it. With that Truman gave the order for the bomb to be used.

ATOMIC ATTACKS

The first atomic bomb was dropped on Hiroshima on the morning of 6 August 1945 by a B-29 bomber flown from the island of Tinian. The bomb killed about 80,000 people more or less instantly; an estimated 50,000 more died from its short- and long-term radiation effects.

Above: Many of the survivors, like this woman from Hiroshima, suffered terrible burns in the atomic attacks.

Nagasaki suffered a similar fate, but with slightly fewer casualties, on 9 August.

There is no doubt that Truman's decision to use the bomb was made in large part in the hope that it would spare lives by making Japan surrender. However, the historical record is also clear that part of the motive was to intimidate the Soviets and lay down a marker for the post-war world.

The Soviets issued their promised declaration of war on the 8th and their forces crashed across the border into Japanese-held Manchuria the next day. Japan's supposedly elite Kwantung Army, outnumbered and outmatched in every category of weaponry, simply fell apart. Manchuria and northern Korea were overrun within days.

THE SURRENDER

Emperor Hirohito now intervened to tell the diehard militarists in his government that the war must be ended. To the last there was the same dithering and failure to face facts at the heart of Japan's government as had helped get Japan into the mess in the first place. This was epitomized in Hirohito's broadcast to his people in which he blandly stated that "the war situation has developed not necessarily to Japan's advantage".

Even so that same day, 15 August, was celebrated by the Allies as VJ-Day. Japan's formal surrender was signed on the US battleship *Missouri* in Tokyo Bay on 2 September.

Below: General MacArthur, backed by a row of Allied representatives, at the surrender ceremony.

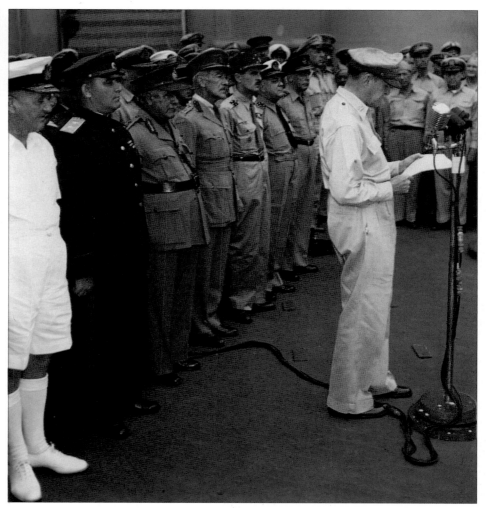

INVASION OF JAPAN

The planned Allied invasion of Japan would have been the largest landing operation in history. Two phases were intended: Operation Olympic against the island of Kyushu in November 1945, and, using bases gained there, Operation Coronet, the final decisive attack on the Kanto Plain on Honshu, near Tokyo, scheduled for March 1946. Casualty estimates varied widely, but typical figures were 400,000 Allied dead (including significant British Empire forces, not just Americans) and more than ten times that number of Japanese.

New Nations Refugees at Amritsar in the last days of pre-independence India.

Dealing with the Defeated Leading Nazis in the dock during the Nuremberg trials.

The Cold War American transport aircraft unloading supplies in Berlin during the Airlift in 1948.

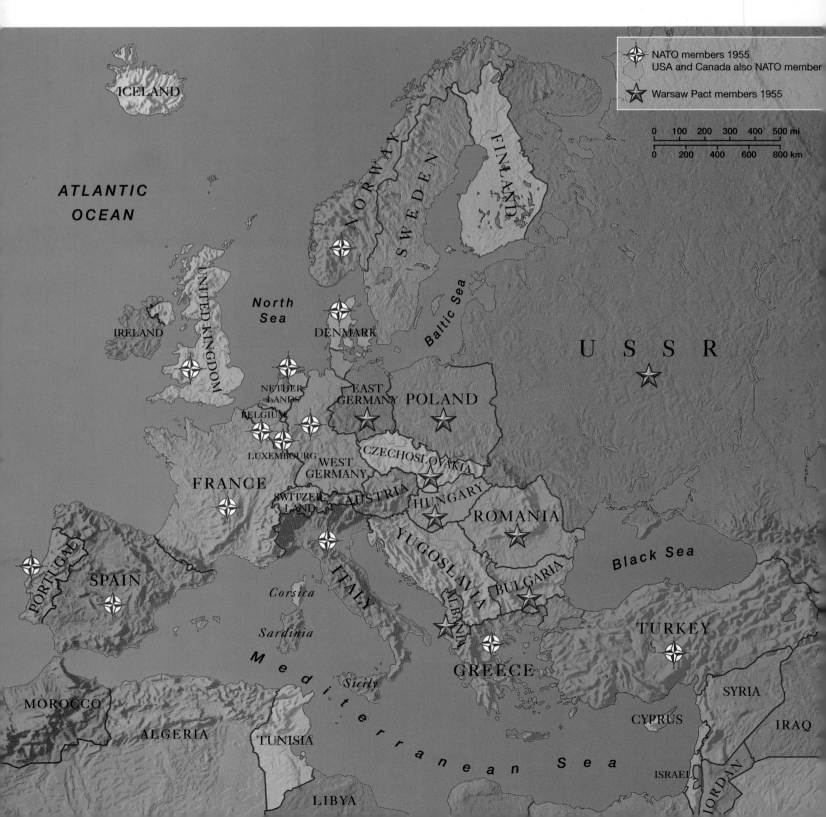

NATO members 1955
USA and Canada also NATO member

Warsaw Pact members 1955

0   100   200   300   400   500 mi
0   200   400   600   800 km

ICELAND

ATLANTIC
OCEAN

NORWAY

SWEDEN

FINLAND

North
Sea

Baltic Sea

IRELAND

UNITED KINGDOM

DENMARK

U S S R

NETHER-
LANDS

EAST
GERMANY

POLAND

BELGIUM

LUXEMBOURG

WEST
GERMANY

CZECHOSLOVAKIA

FRANCE

SWITZER-
LAND

AUSTRIA

HUNGARY

ROMANIA

PORTUGAL

SPAIN

Corsica

ITALY

YUGOSLAVIA

BULGARIA

Black Sea

Sardinia

ALBANIA

TURKEY

Mediterranean

GREECE

Sicily

SYRIA

MOROCCO

CYPRUS

IRAQ

ALGERIA

TUNISIA

Sea

ISRAEL

JORDAN

LIBYA

THE LEGACY OF WAR

No one claimed in 1945 that World War II would become the "war to end all wars", but it did establish that any future war would have different causes. The expansionist militarism that had characterized both Germany and Japan since the early years of the 20th century was discredited for good in the eyes of most German and Japanese people, as was the murderous racism that accompanied it.

For a time after 1945 it also seemed that the US atomic monopoly (in the event lasting only until 1949) would deter attacks on the USA and its friends. However, the mutual suspicions between the USSR and the Western Allies (some of them justified, some not) brought the increasing tension and competition of the Cold War. Although the Cold War itself did not outlast the century, its legacy remains important in the new millennium.

Many of the more controversial methods employed in modern conflicts can trace their history directly to WWII. The resistance movements and similar organizations of the war used tactics familiar 60 years on to freedom fighters and terrorists and, for all their precision weapons, 21st-century air forces still bomb civilians as regularly and with as little scruple as their forebears did.

Dealing with the Defeated Temporary housing being built amid the devastation of Hiroshima.

The Cold War President Truman signs the NATO treaty, committing the USA to the defence of Europe.

Europe Divided German civilians trying desperately to gather coal for fuel on a mine spoil heap.

Casualties and Destruction

World War II was the most brutal conflict in human history, with a death toll several times that of any previous war. Death came to civilians far from the front line, as it did to soldiers, with a dreadful thoroughness never before contemplated.

The human cost of WWII was truly enormous but is still impossible to measure exactly. Even in the early 21st century, when most records have been opened to historical study and most of the bitterness associated with the war has long subsided, no one has been able to calculate exact figures, nor ever will be. The lowest figure that is at all plausible is some 40 million dead, but other estimates go as high as 55 million. Also on top of that huge figure were probably three times as many wounded, of whom many would have to live with pain and disability for the remainder of their lives. And as well as these were the many more still, who were emotionally scarred by their experiences or the loss of loved ones. The weight of suffering was immense.

HARROWING TOLL

There is no question that the losses of the Soviet Union were the greatest of all and that the

Above: A memorial to the children of the Czech village of Lidice, destroyed by the Nazis in 1942.

Eastern Front was the theatre in which the fighting was the largest in scale and the least restrained by moral limitations. The Soviet armed forces lost at least 10 million killed, including a large proportion who died of ill-treatment as prisoners in German hands and many who, once liberated from German captivity or returned to Soviet control by the Western Allies, were sent straight to the GUlag. Soviet civilian deaths amounted to 10 million or more, the largest proportion of these being murdered by Stalin's regime.

Dominating the list of European civilian casualties are the 6 million Jews murdered by the Nazis, who came all too close to their objective of making Europe Jew-free – only around 300,000 Jews from areas that had been Nazi-controlled survived the war.

The country second on the list after the USSR is China, another for which any exact reckoning is impossible. Common estimates are in the range of 10–15 million, of whom 2–3 million were fighters in one or other of the armies.

The major Axis powers both fared badly, though in each case military casualties predominated over civilian. Perhaps 4.5 million German soldiers died and another 2 million civilians. Japan's total casualties were about 2 million. Poland and Yugoslavia both suffered particularly severely. Poland lost some 4–4.5 million, more than half of them Jews, and Yugoslavia over 1.5 million in the country's vicious resistance and civil-war struggle.

Of the major Allied powers, Britain lost some 350,000 dead, considerably fewer than in WWI, and the countries of the British Empire an additional 120,000. In proportion to its population the losses of the USA were by far the lowest of any

Left: A memorial at the former Dachau concentration camp near Munich, one of the first to be set up.

major combatant: approximately 275,000, of whom all but a handful were military personnel.

In addition to the millions killed or injured were the millions more who ended the war as refugees. Even if they did have homes to return to, many had no wish to do this because wartime events or subsequent political changes meant they would be in danger or unwelcome. There may have been as many as 30 million "displaced persons" (as they were known) in Europe at the end of the war and millions more in China.

PHYSICAL DESTRUCTION

As well as the human cost of the war the scale of physical damage was stunning. Even in Britain, which was comparatively lightly bombed and saw no land fighting, hundreds of thousands of homes suffered war damage. In Germany and Japan whole cities were virtually demolished by Allied bombing. In the western

Above: The British War Graves Commission cemetery at El Alamein, seen shortly after the war.

USSR roughly two-thirds of the homes, factories and other resources were destroyed in the fighting or by the scorched-earth policies applied in retreat, first by the Soviets themselves and later by the Germans.

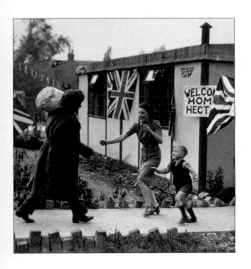

Left: A British soldier returns to his family, in their new "prefab" home, after a four-year absence.

Right: Displaced persons crowding a train in Berlin in June 1945.

Dealing with the Defeated

*Unlike in WWI, when the Allies only occupied part of Germany, in 1945 both
Germany and Japan were occupied and administered by the Allied powers.
International tribunals also tried and punished war criminals in both countries.*

At the Casablanca Conference in January 1943 President Roosevelt had declared (and Prime Minister Churchill agreed) that the Allies would seek the unconditional surrender of Germany and Japan. Later in 1943 Britain, the USA and the USSR established the European Advisory Commission to draw up surrender terms for Germany and to work out occupation arrangements for Germany (and Austria, which the Allies decided should be separated from Germany again) and the minor Axis powers. These plans were eventually agreed by the heads of government at the Yalta and Potsdam conferences in 1945.

Allied Control Commissions were set up to run the occupied Axis countries. In the case of Germany this meant that the country was to be divided into

Above: July 1945, a typical Berlin street scene. Locals trudge past the rubble with their few belongings.

four occupation zones – one each for the USA, UK, USSR and France – and Berlin would also be similarly divided.

Various plans for Japan were considered, including versions with the country divided into Allied zones. Instead, when the time came, General MacArthur was appointed Allied Supreme Commander for the occupation. All of Japan's main islands came under American control, with MacArthur acting almost as a ruling monarch. The Soviets occupied (and would retain as Soviet territory) the Kurile Islands and the southern half of Sakhalin, while the occupation forces of the main Japanese islands included a British Empire contingent.

PUNISHING THE GUILTY

In 1943 the Allies had also announced their intention to punish Nazi war criminals. In the Potsdam declaration in 1945 the process was extended to include Japanese leaders. This resulted in two sets of major international war crimes trials, at Nuremberg and Tokyo, in which some of the most senior figures were tried. In the end 22 Germans and 25 Japanese were tried (indictments in both trials named others who died, were judged unfit to plead or committed suicide). There were also numerous trials conducted by the individual Allied powers of those accused of crimes affecting only one Allied nation.

Left: Temporary housing for civilians in the area blasted by the Hiroshima atomic bomb.

The charges at the major trials included two new concepts in international law, crimes against peace and crimes against humanity, as well as the better-established concept of war crimes in breach of previous internationally agreed standards regarding such things as treatment of prisoners of war. There were three outright acquittals at Nuremberg but none at Tokyo, though some defendants were found not guilty on some of the charges brought against them. Punishments included 19 death sentences and various long terms of imprisonment.

VICTORS' JUSTICE?

Some aspects of the trials were unsatisfactory. Certainly there was an element of victors' justice – for example, Stalin was just as guilty for his invasion of Poland in 1939 and the subse-

Above: General Tojo, Japan's Prime Minister for most of the war, was executed after the Tokyo trials.

quent murders of thousands of Poles as any of the Nazis. And a truly impartial court might well have considered the Anglo-American strategic bombing campaigns as war crimes.

In the Japanese case the defendants were selected and the prosecution evidence slanted so that Emperor Hirohito

and his family were left untainted, because this suited the Allied occupation policies.

Although there has been much discussion since about the legality and fairness of the proceedings, they definitely established the principle that national leaders can be brought to account before the international community and that soldiers everywhere have a duty to disobey unlawful orders. And the evidence at Nuremberg proved beyond all doubt that the Nazis did murder some 6 million Jews among much else, however much some have since tried to deny this. Whatever flaws there may have been, these were valuable precedents.

Below: Top Nazis in the dock at the Nuremberg trials. Hermann Göring (front left) was the most senior figure to stand trial.

Europe Divided

In a famous speech in 1946 Winston Churchill described how Europe had been divided by an Iron Curtain. The suspicions that had hindered the wartime alliance between Britain, the USA and USSR were hardening into something more serious.

Although the war ended in 1945 with Western and Soviet troops in control of respective halves of Europe, very few would have expected this to be a long-lasting state of affairs. Indeed the leading Allied powers, including the Soviets, had issued the so-called Declaration on Liberated Europe at the Yalta Conference in early 1945. This stated that they intended to see democratic governments and free elections in countries they had liberated from German control.

WESTERN EUROPE

There was never any question that these pledges would be fulfilled in Western Europe. The Allied powers had backed governments-in-exile of all

Above: Germans searching through the spoil from a coal mine in a desperate hunt for scarce fuel.

Below: Czech politician Jan Masaryk died in suspicious circumstances after the communist takeover in 1948.

these countries during the war. The removal of the Germans in 1944–5 was followed shortly after by elections. Local communist parties, which had been prominent in the resistance movements to the German occupation, participated fully in these elections and, notably in France and Italy, won a significant number of votes.

It was clear that conditions in Eastern Europe would be different. Even as the Yalta Conference was taking place, the Soviets were already working to ensure that communists would take control in Bulgaria and in March 1945 they set up a communist government in Romania.

THE UNITED NATIONS

The history of the United Nations (UN) dates to the Four Power Declaration (by the USA, UK, USSR and China) in October 1943 that they intended to establish an international organization after the war to maintain "international peace and security". After further discussions the UN was established by the San Francisco Conference in 1945, attended by delegates from 50 countries. Even at that early stage there were problems. Poland was not represented because the USA and USSR did not agree about the composition of a legitimate Polish government.

Right: A US atomic test at Bikini Atoll, 1946. Old warships are placed nearby to assess the blast's power.

Britain (and later the USA) had supported a Polish government-in-exile in London from the early stages of the war but, as the Red Army advanced in 1944, the Soviets put forward an alternative communist group, which they recognized at the end of the year as the provisional government. Some of the "London Poles" did return home in 1945, but they had been removed from government and all opposition silenced by early 1947. During 1947–8 there were further communist takeovers in Hungary and Czechoslovakia.

OPPOSING COMMUNISM

Concerns over these developments and disagreements about how to deal with Germany soon provoked changes on the Anglo-American side. At the start of 1946 President Truman spoke about the need to "get tough with Russia" and other senior figures urged that the USA adopt a policy of "firm and vigilant containment of Russian expansionist tendencies". Winston Churchill's "Iron Curtain" speech followed shortly after and, though he was by then an ex-prime minister, the British government agreed with him.

Since the end of WWII Britain had been helping the Greek government to combat a communist-led civil war, but in early 1947 Britain, in dire economic trouble, told the USA that it could no longer afford to do so.

Right: President Truman addressing the first meeting of the United Nations in June 1945.

Stalin had kept his wartime promise not to interfere in Greece and such external aid as the Greek communists were receiving came from Yugoslavia, which was not at all the same thing as saying it came from Moscow. But this was not clearly understood then in the West.

Instead the USA agreed to take over Britain's role in Greece and also to help Turkey. This policy was summed up in March 1947 by President Truman's promise to "support free peoples" resisting subversion. This was the start of what became known as the Truman Doctrine.

Europe's economies as a whole were still suffering from the destruction of the war years and the particularly severe winter of 1946–7 had not helped. In 1946 Britain and the USA had agreed to stop taking reparations from Germany. By early 1947 they were beginning to consider supporting a German economic recovery as part of a concerted strategy to revive European prosperity. This would also be beneficial to the Americans because of the markets it would create.

Western and Soviet policies were rapidly moving farther apart than ever.

New Nations

Japanese rule in Asia had been brutal and racist but it made a restoration of the European colonies impossible. In the Middle East substantial Jewish immigration after the war also meant that new conditions prevailed.

The wartime slogan of Japan's Greater East Asia Co-Prosperity Sphere had been "Asia for the Asiatics" and, for all the brutality of their subsequent rule, the Japanese triumphs of 1941–2 had largely discredited the former colonial masters. The Anglo-American Atlantic Charter of 1941 had, at American insistence, openly supported the right of people everywhere to choose their own governments – and American policy throughout the war was avowedly anti-colonial. Both of these factors assisted the developing forces of nationalism.

COLONIAL STRUGGLES

In French Indo-China (now Laos, Cambodia and Vietnam), for example, the American Office of Strategic Services sup-

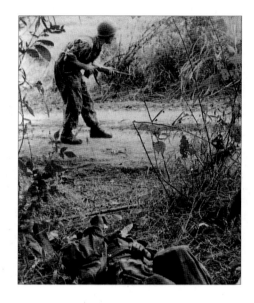

Above: A French soldier in Indo-China in 1951 during the fruitless attempt to maintain French rule.

Below: Refugees in Amritsar, among the millions forced to move because of their religion when India and Pakistan became independent.

ported a Vietnamese nationalist coalition led by the communist Ho Chi Minh during the war. Ho's Viet Minh forces fought against the Japanese and, at the end of the war, proclaimed the existence of a Democratic Republic of Vietnam. France subsequently tried (unsuccessfully) to reimpose colonial rule. Thus began the long conflict, which would only end with the North Vietnamese victory over South Vietnam in 1975.

In the Dutch East Indies the pre-war colonial power also tried and failed to reimpose its control after the war. Here the Japanese had worked with the nationalist leader Achmad Sukarno during the war and in 1944 had promised to grant independence. With help from the Japanese, Sukarno went on to proclaim Indonesia as an independent country in August 1945. This was finally recognized by the Dutch in 1949 after a bitter, armed struggle.

Unlike the Dutch and the French, Britain had substantial forces available to re-occupy Malaya and the other territories that remained under Japanese control in August 1945. However, whether they had been Japanese-occupied at any stage or not, almost all British colonies in Asia quickly gained their independence. In 1939, despite the well-established system of partial self-government, Britain's viceroy in India had declared the country to be

Right: British Indian Army troops fighting in Java in late 1945 against Indonesian nationalists. British forces initially took control in Indonesia after Japan's surrender.

at war with Germany without consulting a single Indian. By 1945 there was no doubt that those days were past, and in August 1947 India and Pakistan became independent.

ISRAEL AND THE ARABS

European rule had also had its day in the Middle East. The pre-war French mandate in Syria was never restored and the country became independent in effect in 1944. Britain's pre-war mandate in Palestine had been troubled by violence between Jews and Arabs and the British authorities; various plans had been proposed for separate and joint Jewish and Arab states.

British control continued as a United Nations' mandate after the war amid growing violence. Jewish immigration and the experience of the Holocaust lent more force to Zionism than previously, while UN attempts to broker a deal between Arabs and Jews came to nothing. In 1948, when the British mandate expired, the state of Israel was proclaimed; Israel had been successfully established by 1949. Perhaps around 700,000 Palestinian Arabs were displaced from their homes, creating a legacy of bitterness that persists into the 21st century.

COMMUNIST CHINA

The biggest of the post-war changes was in China. For all the Allied aid that had been sent to the Nationalists, the Communists had done better out of the war. Their armed forces were better organized and in 1945 they already had an effective presence in most of the supposedly Japanese-controlled areas of the country.

Over the following years, the communists gradually gained the upper hand throughout the country and in 1949 proclaimed the People's Republic of China; the defeated Nationalists withdrew to Taiwan. In the West this looked like an important victory for world communism, as directed from Moscow. In reality the Chinese communists were masters in their own house, but for the moment their success only contributed to the development of Cold War tensions.

Right: David Ben-Gurion, first Prime Minister of Israel.

The Cold War

By 1949 the focus of international affairs was no longer on dealing with the effects of WWII. Instead the USA, USSR and many other nations were preoccupied by a new and, in an era of nuclear weapons, possibly more dangerous conflict, the Cold War.

By the middle of 1947 the relationship between the USA and USSR was already at a low ebb. The two had never entirely trusted each other as wartime allies and things had since got much worse. For the moment the USA still had a monopoly of atomic weapons and could be fairly sure that it and its friends were immune from any direct military attack.

However, Europe's economies were still failing to make any substantial recovery from the disastrous conditions of 1945. In this atmosphere, American leaders feared that communist ideas might make headway. A central part of the problem was that Allied policies had in fact prevented the reconstruction of Germany. Instead, led by the Soviets, the Allies had stripped German industry of much plant and other resources.

Above: Konrad Adenauer, first Chancellor of the new nation of West Germany, is congratulated by a supporter after his election victory in August 1949.

THE MARSHALL PLAN

This all changed with the announcement of the Marshall Plan. By its terms, American aid was to be offered to all the nations of Europe, including the USSR. President Truman and his advisers attached conditions to the aid – among other things countries receiving it would have to submit to American inspections of how the money was being spent – which they correctly calculated would make it unacceptable to the Soviets. They duly rejected it and ensured that their satellites in eastern Europe did so too.

Marshall Plan aid began to flow in 1948 and over $12 billion would be provided to a range of countries until 1951. During these years the European economies grew substantially and levels of prosperity surpassed those of the late 1930s. International trade also revived, to the benefit not just of the Europeans but also of the American economy. And finally, because they had been forced to work together to decide how the aid should be split up, the European nations began the process of economic co-operation that would lead to the establishment in 1957 of the European Economic Community and in time to the present-day European Union.

NEW GERMANIES

In March 1948 the USA, Britain and France agreed to merge their occupation zones of Germany into a single entity. In June they introduced a new

Left: Unloading transport aircraft at Tempelhof airfield, June 1948, during the Berlin Blockade.

GEORGE MARSHALL

General Marshall (1880–1959) was Chief of Staff of the US Army from 1939 to the end of the war. He is regarded as the main organizer of the US victory in WWII. First, in 1939–41, he substantially expanded and updated his service and laid the ground for the greater expansion that followed. Throughout the war he worked hard to maintain the principles of "Germany first" and that Germany should be defeated by a direct cross-Channel invasion. After the war he served as Secretary of State, helping devise and implement the Foreign Assistance Act, which came to be known as the Marshall Plan.

currency for the whole area to replace the Hitler-era Reichsmarks that were still in use.

Since the main aim of Soviet policy in Europe after the war was to ensure that Germany could never again dominate the continent, any measures that presaged a German economic revival were seen as threatening. The Soviet response to the Allied currency reforms and other measures was to close all road and rail routes to the Allied sectors in Berlin. This Berlin Blockade is commonly seen as the first clear confrontation of the Cold War.

The Soviets presumably hoped that the Allies would back down over their plans for Germany. They had not reckoned on the ability of the Allies to supply the city by air. Hundreds of American and British aircraft made daily transport flights into the city carrying everything that the Berliners needed. Thus supplied, the city held out until the Soviets relented in 1949.

By then the Cold War had truly begun. In 1949 West and East Germany were established as new countries, with the first elections in the West in August. In April, 12 countries, including Britain, the USA and Canada, signed the North Atlantic Treaty, agreeing that an attack on any one would be regarded as an attack on all. This NATO alliance was an open commitment by the USA not to return to the policies of isolationism that had prevailed before WWII. On the other side there was a new threat. In August 1949 the Soviets tested their first atomic weapon and would establish their own military alliance of Soviet-bloc countries, the Warsaw Pact, in the 1950s.

The Cold War competition between NATO and the Warsaw Pact and the accompanying nuclear balance of terror would dominate international affairs for the next forty years. The great issues that had brought about WWII were now relegated to history.

Above: General George Marshall in US Army uniform late in the war.